Triathlete in Transition

an inspirational, commonsense guide for the novice triathlete

BY RAY FAUTEUX, AUTHOR OF..

"Ironstruck ... The Ironman Triathlon Journey,"

"Ironstruck? 500 Ironman Triathlon Questions and Answers,"

"Lifestruck ... A Better Way For Today's Youth."

INTRODUCING GUEST EXPERTS....

KEVAN MacNAUGHTON – 26 years with "The Bike Shop"
GRANT MOLYNEUX – Triathlete, coach, author
SHELLY MacGREGOR – Massage Therapist
DEREK COOK – Naturopathic Doctor
JEFF THOMLINSON –Trinity Yoga

FEATURING..

STEVE KING – The voice of Ironman Canada and Ultra-athlete
TERRY LAUGHLIN – Creator of *Total Immersion Swimming*

Triathlete in Transition

Printed by Blitzprint

ISBN: 978-0-9813616-0-4

CONTENTS

** Chapter features guest expert.

ACKNOWLEDGMENTS

Thank you...

When I first considered writing this book I had every intention of following the guidelines I set in place for myself when I created Ironstruck the website, and my first three books.

I would not write about a subject that I did not have experience with myself at one point or other during my life or during my athletic career.

I always thought that to do so would be a disservice to the people who took the time to read what I had to say. At the same time, it limited me as to what I could pass on that might be helpful to others when it came to topics I knew little or nothing about.

On that note, I would like to thank the special people who have agreed to share their knowledge with the readers of this book, especially the guest writers for "Triathlete in Transition."

First of all, I would like to thank Kevan, who actually inspired me to search out guest writers when I asked him to explain all about road bikes and triathlon bikes and what the novice triathlete should take into consideration when making their bike purchase as they venture into the world of triathlon. He explained it so eloquently that out of the blue I said, "would you like to write that part of the book for me?"

So thanks, Kevan. Thanks for helping me out now, and also 25 years ago when you shared your knowledge and expertise and were instrumental in helping me cross the finish line of Ironman Hawaii in 1984. I have never forgotten.

It was so great being part of the Ironman Calgary 70.3 Expo because I had the opportunity to meet so many talented and special people.

Shelly, I knew pretty well right away that I would ask you to be the expert on massage therapy for the triathlete and how it can benefit them as they take on new physical challenges. You have the knowledge and personality that make you a natural to give positive and informative input on the subject. Thank you so much.

Derek, it was very enlightening to have the opportunity to speak to you about Naturopathic medicine and how it can have such a profound effect on the health and well-being of all of us. Your passion for your career of choice is so evident that I have no doubt that you will be hugely successful as you begin your practice in Calgary. Thank you for sharing that passion with the readers of "Triathlete in Transition."

I hear so much about Yoga, but know nothing about it and how it might benefit the athlete. Jeff, you were the natural choice to teach me and the readers of this book about the benefits of Yoga. Your experience with top level pro athletes and as one of the pioneers in the earliest days of triathlon make you a great choice.

Grant, what can I say? You were right there with me in Hawaii back in 1984 when the sport of triathlon was still in its infancy. What strikes me the most is how those early years had such a profound impact on the direction our lives have taken today. It truly was the start of a remarkable journey that's certainly not over yet. It's pretty special to me that you are part of this book.

Like so many other aspiring triathletes around the world I struggled mightily with the concept of swimming. With triathlon, it's about much more than just swimming from one end of the pool to the other. It's also about swimming in the open water with confidence and with a technique that conserves energy for the biking and running. Total Immersion was a Godsend to me and for the first time I truly *enjoyed* swimming in a triathlon rather than just trying to survive it. I'm sure I speak for many triathletes around the world when I say "thank you, Terry, for what you bring to the sport and for what you are bringing to Triathlete in Transition".

Steve, I don't even know where to start. So many times in the late 80's and early 90's I reached the crest of the hill on Main Street and heard your resonating voice calling to me and giving me the strength to reach the finish line of Ironman Canada. Athletes from Australia, Germany, U.K., U.S, Japan, and dozens of other countries around the world have experienced the magic of your passion for what you do. I can't even begin to tell you what an honor it is to have your words of wisdom in this book.

I'll always remember the day I walked into Tri-It and first met Rose Serpico, who along with Brian Del Castilho, shares ownership of Tri-It Multi-Sport. I will never forget how Rose said "yes" without hesitation when I asked her if she would like to carry my newly published book "Ironstruck ... the Ironman Triathlon Journey" in her store. Tri-It became the first retailer to carry my book, and the rest as they say, is history. It seems so perfect that Rose is gracing the cover of "Triathlete in Transition". Just five days before the cover shoot, Rose crossed the finish line of Ironman Canada, and is an inspiration to so many who are about to begin their own triathlon journey. Thanks Rose, I will never forget your kindness and your undying faith in "Ironstruck".

Come and visit the finest triathlon store in the country and say hello to Rose and Brian at 2640 Parkdale Boulevard NW in Calgary or visit their website at www.tri-it.ca.

My deepest thanks go out as well to Margaret Jezierska, whose deft work on the cover art and design has made this book as appealing as it is informational, and to Jordan Bryden, who handled the photography. Jordan, you did such a great job on such short notice, and you were a pleasure to work with. I think you have a real future in photography as well as being a world class triathlete.

Cindy, without your patience and calmness I would never have made it past my first book. So many people around the world have benefited from "Ironstruck", and without you it would never have been born. You are an integral player in the creation of Triathlete in Transition and by bringing us all together you are helping create a book we can all be proud of.

Thank you all, and perhaps together we can make a difference in the lives of people by convincing them that embracing a life of health, fun, and fitness through triathlon will have a postive and everlasting effect on not just their physical wellbeing, but every aspect of their lives.

ABOUT THE AUTHOR

The author is 60 years old and was born in Northern Manitoba, but spent most of his preteen and teen years growing up and going to school in Vancouver. He currently calls Calgary, Alberta home where he has now resided for over 25 years.

In 1976, while watching the Olympic Summer Games in Montreal, the author was inspired to give up smoking and an all-around unhealthy lifestyle and venture into the world of running. It was a fortuitous decision that would change the course of his life.

He reached the finish line of his first marathon less than a year later. In the coming years, over 30 marathons, a couple of 50-mile road races, many shorter road races and entry into 14 Ironman Triathlons would follow.

Inspired by the 1982 televised version of Ironman Hawaii, he was instantly drawn to the challenge of crossing that finish line in Kona, despite having a healthy fear of the water and no idea how to swim.

In 1984, after a year of relentless thrashing and splashing in local pools, crossing the finish line in Kona went from being a deep-rooted desire and dream to a reality. The transition changed the course of the author's life forever, and brought him where he is today, writing this book for you. For you, the novice triathlete who also has goals and dreams and distant finish lines to cross that perhaps seem out of your reach.

This is his fourth book. The very first book was called "Ironstruck ... The Ironman Triathlon Journey". The author was trying to capture in one word what happens to people – and what happened to him – when something they see, hear, or read inspires them to change the course of their lives forever. Something that fires the passion we all have inside, but which might lay dormant and unrealized for years, and often for a lifetime, unless we are fortunate enough to be moved, inspired, and awakened to our full potential.

That word became "Ironstruck".

Ironstruck initially began as the website, ironstruck.ca. A South African triathlete who was using the Ironstruck website as a guide for his very first Ironman in Mandella Bay suggested that the author should write a book for the novice Ironman. As a result, Ironstruck the book was born.

In the years that followed, it seemed to the author that people who were taking on the challenge of their first Ironman were in great need of information. Soon questions about the Ironman and triathlon in general were arriving at the website Ironstruck.ca from all over the world and it became apparent that what people really needed was somewhere to turn for the answers to their questions. That resulted in the writing of one of the few (or perhaps the only) Ironman Triathlon question and answer books in the world. Ironstruck? 500 Ironman Triathlon Questions and Answers" became the author's second book.

During book signings he had the opportunity to speak with many teachers, doctors and other health care practitioners, and began to get a sense of how a lack of proper diet and fitness was reaching epidemic proportions among the youth of North America. The urge to help in some small way inspired the writing of book number three, "Lifestruck ... A Better Way For Today's Youth". "Lifestruck" is intended to inspire preteens and teens to make healthy food choices and to embrace fitness and sport as a way of life.

Presently the sport of triathlon continues to explode onto the world sporting scene. It seems like there is no end in sight to its popularity as more and more people are beginning to realize the wide range of benefits that are there for the taking if they adopt triathlon as their sport, and through it, embrace a healthier way of living.

It seemed to the author that many of these people who are hearing the clarion call of triathlon, doubt themselves and their ability to make the transition from fit to unfit, unhealthy to healthy, or maybe from a runner to a triathlete. Perhaps they have yet to experience that one luminous moment in their lives that ignites that flame; the moment when they are indeed, "Ironstruck".

It's not just about a sport. It's about evolving and reaching new heights on so many levels and accomplishing great physical, emotional, and mental feats that for so long have seemed beyond the grasp of so many.

The author has no doubt that triathlon has the power to change the lives of people all over the world, and often all that's needed is a little encouragement and inspiration to jump-start their new journey.

It is this belief that has inspired "Triathlete in Transition".

There is one thing that has become abundantly clear to the author over the years. The ability to participate in sport and to basically "play" has the remarkable power to spur growth on so many levels. It builds self-esteem, promotes great health and wellbeing, accentuates mental acuity, forms amazing friendships, vitalizes communities, and creates a bond between people that transcends ethnic boundaries and through sport we truly can become the "family of man".

It is this realization that has convinced the author to be a proud supporter of "Right To Play", an amazing organization that gives kids from North America to the farthest corners of the world the opportunity to just be kids and grow and thrive through participation in sports.

We all care and we all want to help others, but often don't know where to direct that help where it will do the most good. Perhaps by giving children the gift of *play* we can make the world a better place for generations to come. I hope you join with me in supporting this great cause. Visit righttoplay.com and learn more about this amazing organization that is supported by professional athletes, Olympic athletes, and caring people all over the world.

INTRODUCTION

Each of us – everyone on this earth – has something in common. When we first enter this world, we have no say about the family, the city, the country, or the culture we find ourselves immersed in as we grow and develop. We have little recourse as children as far as the quality of our lives throughout the crucial formative years of physical, mental, and emotional development. Of course there are those who are athletically gifted and enjoy a lifetime of health and fitness that is rooted in a childhood that included a variety of sports and a healthy lifestyle. Often these individuals become professional athletes or Olympic champions.

However, many children are not athletically inclined and even if by nature they do love sports, might never be quite good enough to make the school team. Or perhaps their family dynamic holds them back from having the opportunity to embrace sports and fitness as a way of life. Either way, when kids are left out, it can often be a big blow to self-esteem and self-confidence. I can still remember kids from my high school years who were scared witless and mortified every time they had to put on gym shorts and go to Physical Education classes. Being fit and playing went from being fun to something they dreaded, and as a result, being fit and physically active was replaced by less healthy alternatives.

It seems to be an undeniable truth that for the most part, the way we leave our school years is the way we enter adulthood. If we have low self-esteem and poor health and fitness habits when we are young, it often carries over and blends seamlessly into the adult years. I know that with all my heart, because it happened to me.

Sure, we eventually get married, have our own families, and build our futures and careers the best we can with the tools we have. Against all odds, many people are amazingly successful in their careers and are truly remarkable, caring parents. Despite what they may have endured in their childhood, many adults show remarkable strength and resilience in making the most of the cards they have been dealt in this life. To all who know them, these people are amazing success stories and are living the good life.

At least on the outside.

On the inside, hidden from most of the world, there is often a struggle taking place. It's a struggle whose roots go back to the days in school when many watched from the side-lines of life and never truly got to participate. They watched as others seemed to breeze through their youth surrounded by friends, athletic success and all that they yearned for themselves, but were denied because of life circumstances out of their control.

However, something remarkable happened about 3 decades ago that has opened a window of opportunity for many people to find that certain something that always seemed to be just out of their grasp--a bridge too far and a finish line too distant for them to reach.

In the late 70's an upsurge in running as a pastime took place and as the 1980's unfolded, a "running craze" began to sweep across North America. At the same time, the acceptance of women onto the world running scene took root. It took that long for the women's marathon to be accepted into the Olympic Games. I ran in marathons in the late 1970's that only had one or two women entries, and sometimes there were none.

I believe it's safe to say that when John Collins and his buddies dreamed up the very first Ironman Triathlon in the late 1970's, they had no idea the effect it would have on so many people around the world decades later. Of course many fine athletes have been drawn into the sport but triathlon has also impacted people who are not necessarily athletes, but rather those who are searching for the key to whatever it is that seems to be missing in their lives.

The sport of triathlon has opened many doors for many people, yet there are still many who remain on the sidelines of life who have yet to take that first tentative step toward finding their true limits on so many levels. For some it is difficult to bridge that gap from mediocrity and the sameness of everyday life and into a journey of spectacular self-discovery and personal accomplishment.

My motivation behind writing this book – along with the input of some amazingly talented and knowledgeable guest experts – is to help you bridge that gap, and hopefully inspire you to step into the limelight and realize that you are as capable and deserving as anyone of benefiting from the positive, life-changing impact the sport of triathlon is having on so many.

You will not find complicated training programs in this book, or technical terms that will leave you baffled, unsure, and doubtful if you have what it takes to begin your triathlon journey.

You will not find glossy images gracing the pages of my plain little book.

There are only two images that are truly important when it comes to this book. It's the self-image you have of yourself now and the buffed-up, shiny self-image you will reflect when you cross the finish line of a triathlon one day down the road and realize your life has just taken on a new, healthy, vibrant direction.

Many people spend much of their lives trying to find out who they are, with little success. My hope is to inspire you to create a "new you" and then you can stop looking and start living.

For so many, the mantra is the same. "Let me grow, let me live" – and now that they see the opportunity and challenge in front of them – "let me tri".

"THE CATERPILLAR THOUGHT

THE WORLD WAS OVER,

BUT THEN BECAME

A BEAUTIFUL BUTTERFLY"

– proverb

1. THE ALLURE OF TRIATHLON

Chances are that a triathlon is a long way from anything you have ever attempted in your life. Possibly you don't have an athletic bone in your body, but the lure of triathlon is pulling you in for several reasons. Perhaps you have done some running and entered a few road races and want to ramp it up a notch and take your first shot at a triathlon. One way or the other, you are intrigued by the concept of becoming a triathlete.

Regardless of whether you are male, female, mid-twenties, middle-aged, overweight, out of shape, a smoker, or the poster-person for every before picture in the world of "this will make you morph from this to that" advertising, you have this feeling deep down that it's time for a change. You wouldn't even be holding this book in your hands right now if you were not at least a little bit interested and curious in the possibility of changing the course of your life in some profound way.

There's a very good chance that you have friends, relatives, or co-workers that have suddenly become people you hardly recognize anymore. It seems like over-night they have more bounce in their step and are more likely to choose tofu and salad over burgers and fries these days. Possibly your work lunch breaks have become solitary affairs as your usual Barista buddy has suddenly developed this habit of heading out the door for a noon-time "training run." Training run! What's going on around here?

So there you are at the corner coffee shop all by yourself trying to decide which of the $5.00 creamy-topped fat-bombs will get you through the rest of the day. More and more you see people out running all over the city on summer weekends. Signs keep popping up that shout out: **"CAUTION! TRIATHLON IN PROGRESS!**

Then one day your curiosity gets the best of you, and you stop and watch as biker after biker goes flying past with tires humming across the asphalt with spokes glistening in the sunlight. You are intrigued because many of the cyclists don't appear to be the slim, buff athletes you thought they would be.

AND THERE GOES YOUR COFFEE BUDDY! Suddenly it hits you. Hey! Her butt used to be bigger than mine!

Somehow it inspires you, and at first you laugh it off as you go home and look into the mirror at a body that is showing with inescapable clarity the results of years of the "good" life – or perhaps more accurately, years of over-indulgence and neglect in the form of improper diet and a sedentary, listless lifestyle devoid of much in the way of physical exercise.

At least until now...

You find yourself being pulled in, and you don't know it yet, but your life journey may soon be taking a road less traveled that will forever change the way others see you, but more importantly, how you perceive yourself.

2. IN THE BLINK OF AN EYE

"If I had known I was going to live this long, I'd have taken better care of myself." – Eubie Blake, at 100 years old.

You might wonder if the time is right for you to take the leap into this fascinating new world called triathlon.

Often there will be moments of clarity when you know it *is* the right time, but always seem to find a reason to put it off for now. How do I fit it into my work schedule? What about my social life? What about my family – would it be selfish of me to spend this time on myself and not with my family?

The funny thing is, there is not one aspect of your life that will not actually benefit from you choosing a fitter, healthier lifestyle. In effect, it might just be the most loving, "selfish" thing you can do for those who are closest to you.

The fact that you are about to explore new boundaries and improve yourself on so many levels will help ensure you have the best chance at a long and healthy life. What better gift could you give to people who care about you and need you?

For years now big companies have been encouraging their employees to live healthier lives. Some companies have their own fitness facilities or offer employees reduced-rate fitness club memberships. Long ago they figured out that a healthy, confident employee is less likely to miss work, will be a happier employee, and will be more efficient at their job. To take it a step further, improving your fitness level and overall health will improve pretty well every aspect of your life.

Your teenage kids might be in momentary shock to see mom hitting the road on her spiffy new bike, or dad heading out the door for a run before breakfast, but I can almost guarantee they will be among your biggest supporters when you cross the finish line of a triathlon one day in the future.

Deep down you will know if it's the right time for you or not.

As clear as day I can remember picking up my wife and first child as I brought them home from the hospital just days after my son was born. I drove at about 10 mph because I was afraid that 6lb. 8oz. package might break or something. Now when I meet him and his new wife for coffee I'm suddenly looking across at a thirty-something, 190 pound man.

"Where did you take my baby boy and what did you do with him?" Holy crap!

Just remember, that time marches on and in the blink of an eye you will find that years have been swallowed up and they are never coming back. Now is the time to build amazing new memories that will sustain you for the rest of your life.

Someone once asked, "why do people have to die?" "To make life more important" was the answer they got.

It's so true when you think about it. We have a certain amount of time to make our mark in this world. If you put it off too long, you will simply run out of time. We have only a limited amount of time to realize dreams we once thought impossible, and to soar with the eagles. Most of us never come close to using the full scope of the abilities we have been gifted with. Every single day we have the opportunity to take our lives in a new direction and it's very true that "today is the first day of the rest of our lives."

Far too often we look outwardly for the reasons why our lives are not as fulfilling as we feel they should be, but ultimately what we do with our remaining time on this earth is up to us and nobody else.

3. IS IT TOO LATE FOR ME?

If it's in your heart to make a positive change in your life – whatever it happens to be – then I don't believe it's ever too late. Our bodies are ticking clocks, and we can set the wake-up alarm to go off anytime we like. However lost days, weeks, and years are never coming back and the hands of time only go one way, so it makes sense to look toward to your future and make the most of it. Dwelling on a past that has been less than perfect serves no good purpose and can be a vexation to the spirit. It's never too late to change the course of your life for the better.

Over the past several years since creating ironstruck.ca and writing books on the subject of triathlon, I have come across some amazing people. Some I have met in person, some I have chatted with through emails, and some I have encountered while doing research. Although my purpose with this book and Ironstruck in general is to motivate and inspire others to become more than they ever thought possible on many, many levels, I am continually inspired by the incredible stories of people I have encountered along the way.

So you think it might be too late for you? Well, I just have to tell you this story about Wally, who lives in the United States.

Like many people, Wally retired when he was 65 years old. Wally was never athletic and found that he had tons of time on his hands so decided to take up running. He did that for a few years and really liked it so at 70 years old he began to enter races so he could compete..

Wally went on to set age-group records in his state for several different distances. Well, he didn't stop there. He became world masters champion in several running events in the 90-95 age group and then the 95-100 age group.

The last I heard of Wally, he was quite active and back to looking after beehives in his backyard. At the time, he was well over 100 years old.

So whenever you think it's too late for you, think about Wally. Think about all the possibilities you have locked inside of you just waiting to get out. The true potential of so many people often goes unused because nobody ever believed in them or gave them that little push to encourage them to take the first small step in their journey of true self-discovery.

Maybe the story of Wally will do it for you, or maybe this book will do it for you, but regardless, it is never too late to become more than you are, and to realize just how much you are capable of if you just give yourself a chance.

4. FAT, UNFIT, AND UN-ATHLETIC

Is that all that's stopping you?

If your heart is set on making changes and giving triathlon a try, then being overweight is not an impossible hurdle to overcome. It has been proven over and over again that the spirit of triathlon and the opportunity to be a part of it has inspired many people facing adversity to make a big change in their lives.

Once a person makes it a priority to eat smarter while at the *same time* adopting a life-style of fitness, amazing changes begin to take place in not only their body chemistry and physical make-up, but also in their self-esteem and confidence. It has a ripple effect as one begins to feed on the other and before long you will never want to go back to the way things were. What you are really doing is beginning an entirely new and exciting chapter in your life. Of course it won't be easy. However, it most likely took you many, many years to get to where you are, but it won't take nearly as long to turn things around and the lifelong rewards are well worth the effort.

It's a pretty well known fact that you can be on the best diet in the world, but it's only when you include physical activity along with a smarter way of eating that you achieve the dramatic and long-lasting results.

As far as being "un-athletic," what exactly does that mean anyway?

There are very few adults who do not have the skill to ride a bike. As a kid you probably rode your bike all over the place. Chances are, you are not a complete stranger to running either. I'm sure you ran to the store, ran from the neighborhood bully, ran to the park, ran to school, or ran across the lawn. My point is, the ability to bike and run are often *built-in* from the glory days of our youth, regardless of whether we were ever athletic enough to be part of a school team.

If you take up triathlon, you will simply be honing the skills and ability you have always had, that have never truly gone away. They simply need to be awakened from their long slumber. Of course you will be on a sleeker, faster bike than you have most likely ever ridden, but with time and practice you will hone your balance and bike-handling skills and learn how to get the most out of your bike.

Pretty well everyone knows how to walk and run. All you are really doing when you take up triathlon is extending the distance you can run, bike, and swim by becoming fitter over the course of your training. Our bodies are truly miraculous and will adapt to grow stronger and more toned as we begin to make more physical demands on it. There is a lot of truth to the words "use it or lose it."

Our bodies are capable of so much, but require our increased physical efforts to give it a reason to continually re-build and tone muscles, keep the blood flowing smoothly through un-constricted veins, and to increase our lung capacity.

Swimming is a learned skill, and for many a completely foreign one, but it is very possible to become an excellent swimmer at any age. You are in for a treat, because later on in the book you will have insight from Terry Laughlin, who has inspired many through the "Total Immersion" swimming concept to become confident, proficient swimmers.

Many people can't seem to get their head around the fact that they can be bigger than most people and appear "overweight" and yet still maintain a high level of fitness. Everyone has a different body composition and possibly you will never get "super-skinny" but at the same time eventually get very fit and do very well in the triathlon arena.

I just want to pass on an email I received a few years ago. I have told many people this story because it is truly inspiring and speaks for many who might not be the most awesome physical specimens on the planet, but yet have it in their hearts to make a change in the direction their lives are headed.

> *I live in Swakopmund, Namibia. I'm 39 years old. Within a year I went from fat to fit enough to complete Ironman South Africa in 16h12 mins and 39 seconds enjoying every minute of it. I gave up smoking and my whole outlook on life changed. Once you've done an Ironman, you can do anything!! I didn't lose a whole lot of weight – was refueling too much, but stumbling into your site "Ironstruck" changed my life forever. Thanks, so much!*

> *My success was also in part to the last week before the race. There it is VERY important to rest, eat properly – lots of veggies, pasta, and fruit and of course good proteins.*

> *Do NOT eat too much and definitely stay off all processed foods, white flour, Trans fats.*

> – Elinor

Elinor has put it so eloquently that it just has to inspire you, and it was very moving for me to have her write that something I wrote "changed her life forever", but in truth it was *Elinor* who changed her life forever, and all I did was add a bit of fuel to the spark that was always within her waiting to be ignited. There is no reason you cannot begin your own life-changing journey at this very moment.

Melissa, a fitness specialist and registered dietitian, had this to say in a recently published health and fitness article. It reinforces Elinor's experience and how Elinor's spectacular results show that being fit, healthy, and successful in athletic pursuits is not something necessarily reserved for only the "super-slim".

"Quite a few people out there assume because they are thin, they are healthy. But if they are sedentary, they may have poor heart health indicators and have high stress lives which contribute to heart disease. On the other hand, some people on the heavier side are very active, so their cholesterol levels, heart rates and their blood pressure is within ideal ranges. These are much better signs of cardiovascular health than just being thin or overweight. Being sedentary is a risk to your health."

Thanks to Melissa Aubertin-Coutu who manages Sukha Yoga and Nutrition Center in St. Catherines, Ontario.

5. PUBLIC WORKOUTS EMBARRASS ME

It may surprise you to be reading some of the things you are reading in this book. It might not be what you expect from a triathlon book, but to my way of thinking, it does none of us any good to dodge the real issues that are like anchors holding us down. In order to make real changes perhaps it's time to get those roadblocks out in the open so we can kick them out the door and begin to make positive changes in our lives.

This topic is something that is an issue for many people. In fact it is so much of an issue that many give up without even trying and accept their lot in life and pass from this world without ever realizing just how amazing they are and the great things they are truly capable of.

They feel because they are older, unfit, inept, or overweight, that they simply should never be seen in the gyms, swimming pools, or on the bike-paths of the world. They do not fit the image of how many people perceive "athletes" to be, so feel self-conscious about squeezing into a form-fitting pair of cycling shorts, or spiffy running gear.

Sure, it's not going to be easy to bite the bullet and take your over-sized, life-worn, or unfit body out into the athletic world for everyone to see.

Yes, there are those who are self-absorbed, uncharitable, and unaware of the heroic effort they are witnessing, who may think you are odd, disgusting, laughable, or any number of things, but don't believe for a minute that this is the prevailing attitude that you will encounter.

Over the years I have run thousands of kilometers, spent hours and hours in the pool, and biked more miles than I can remember. On occasion I would come across someone in the course of my training who was overweight and out of shape and obviously struggling with every foot-fall, every pedal stroke, or every single length of the pool.

Did I think they looked ridiculous, odd, or disgusting?

Not in this lifetime.

To me they looked *courageous*.

I believe their heavy breathing is a badge of honor. They have taken up the challenge to better themselves and don't care what anyone thinks.

Yes, they looked courageous.

Better yet, every single year triathlon inspires more and more sedentary, unfit people to take to the running paths, swimming pools and highways of the world, and you will not be alone on your journey of self-discovery.

No, it won't be easy at first to get yourself out there, but with each passing day and each small victory your self-confidence will grow and you will feel pride and not embarrassment when you head out that door for your next training session or perhaps your very first triathlon.

6. PICK A RACE

Pick a race? Why would you pick a race before you even lace up your running shoes for the first time, or learn how to swim?

Chances are that you seldom if ever get in your car without having a destination in mind. When you have a predetermined destination you can plan the route that will ultimately get you where you want to go, and at the same time will know approximately how long it will take to get there.

Well, doing a triathlon is no different. This is especially true if it's your very first one. If you have a goal to shoot for it's far easier to stay committed and to prepare with a purpose. It's also important to have a time-frame that meshes with your level of ability and the degree of difficulty of the triathlon you are preparing for.

The triathlon you have in mind might be a few months or a few years away. It doesn't really matter how far away it is. What is truly important is to allow yourself enough time to go into the race knowing that you are properly prepared.

For example, when I witnessed my very first triathlon on television it happened to be the 1982 Hawaii Ironman. I knew almost right away that I wanted to cross that finish line in Kona one day. Back then, there were no shorter races around, so basically it was the Ironman or nothing.

My goal was to enter the Ironman two years later in 1984 because I didn't know how to swim and had to learn to swim well enough to make it through the 2.4 miles in Kona harbor. I also had to get back on a bike as I hadn't been on one since grade school. For me to jump into the 1983 Ironman would have been unrealistic and most likely a huge mistake.

It was an immense help that I could always focus on the finish line in Kona whenever the going got tough over the long months of training, and it sustained me and kept me motivated to never lose sight of my Hawaii dream.

Today those who are new to the sport have many choices when they decide they want to enter the world of triathlon. The days are long gone when the Ironman was the only option. Yes, there are still those who jump right into the Ironman as their first triathlon, but for the majority of novice triathletes, it makes much more sense to ease into the sport and increase the distances they compete in as their self-confidence, conditioning, and athletic ability improves.

There are so many possibilities open to you when it comes to choosing a triathlon that will suit you best. Perhaps the swim portion of a triathlon is making you hesitant about giving the sport a try. However, there is a solution for you.

TRY A TRI: This race is perfect if you are a bit nervous about the swim leg of a triathlon. There is no set distance for a "try a tri" but races of this type focus on letting people take part in and complete their first triathlon. The swim is normally quite short and most seem to be in the 300 to 400 meter range. It's a very doable distance and if you like, you can even do the breast-stroke for the entire swim. Always keep in mind however, that a long, smooth front crawl is your ultimate goal for your triathlon swim.

If swimming in the open water worries you a bit at first, then find a "try a tri" that has a pool swim. From there you can progress to a "try a tri" that has a short open water swim as opposed to a pool swim.

Normally the bike portion will be around 15 kilometers and the run will be in the 3 kilometer range. It's the perfect way to experience this great sport for the first time.

FORM A RELAY TEAM: If you are still in the process of learning how to swim and are not quite ready to take on your first individual triathlon, consider forming a relay team. If you feel you're not quite ready for the swim or bike, then perhaps you can do the run portion of the race and find two friends who can do the swim and bike legs. You could attempt a different leg each time as you work on improving your fitness and skill levels. By taking part in a relay you will have more options as to what length of race you can do as you are only doing one discipline and not all three. Once you gain confidence and become more proficient at swimming, biking, and running, you will be able to do a short tri all on your own. Also, by being part of a relay team, you will get a feeling for what the sport is all about and it will inspire you to continue improving.

SPRINT TRIATHLON: This would be the natural progression from a "try a tri". A sprint triathlon normally involves a swim of anywhere from a 500 meters to 1000 meters, a 20 kilometer bike, and a 5 kilometer run. Once again, these are not standard distances and will vary from race to race, but will normally be shorter than the Olympic distance and longer than a "try a tri". If you cannot find a "try a tri" in your area, then a "sprint triathlon" would be the logical choice if you are a complete beginner.

OLYMPIC DISTANCE: The Olympic distance is a set distance regardless of where you happen to live in the world. The swim is 1500 meters, followed by a 40 kilometer bike, and a 10 kilometer run. Whether an Olympic distance triathlon is in the Summer Olympic Games or in your city, this is the standard distance.

As you get into the longer races such as this one, you can normally expect the swim to be in the open water as opposed to a pool. For one thing it's far easier for race organizers to manage as pool swims require lap-counters and many different heats as pools can only accommodate a limited amount of swimmers at one time.

It's a very doable distance for the novice triathlete who is a competent swimmer, but if you are nervous about the swim, a shorter triathlon would be a perfect choice to start out with. As you gain confidence and experience you can enter longer races.

THE HALF-IRONMAN: This is also a set distance and includes a 1.9 kilometer swim, followed by a 90 kilometer bike and a 21.1 kilometer run. Once you get into triathlons of this distance you will require more endurance and of course, a lot more training time under your belt.

THE IRONMAN: This is a set distance all over the world, and includes a 3.86 kilometer swim, followed by a 180.25 kilometer bike and a 42.195 kilometer run. In my mind, this is the greatest endurance race in the world.

There are longer races out there and races that are very challenging in their own right, but the Ironman distance is still the greatest race in the world for one main reason.

It's within the reach of ordinary people who hear the challenge of the Iron Gods and are truly "Ironstruck". It's extremely challenging and difficult, yet at the same time, possible for so many if only they believe in themselves and are prepared to do whatever it takes to reach the Ironman finish line.

There are people out there who envision the Ironman finish line, and it's that dream that sustains them as they put in the hours, weeks, months, and even years of training.

So pick a race. Set your sights on a goal and envision yourself crossing that finish line regardless of how long the race is. As you prepare, never let go of that thought and you will feel the true power of a passion – of a dream – and how it can give you wings and lift you as it gets closer and closer to becoming a reality.

7. FIRST THINGS FIRST

There are several things to consider before plunging head first into the world of triathlon.

SEE YOUR DOCTOR: There are several reasons why you should visit your doctor before you begin your triathlon journey. First of all, if you do happen to be unfit, overweight, and very new to any form of physical exercise it would be wise to have your doctor give you a complete physical examination. Chances are any doctor would endorse your efforts to include a better diet and regular fitness into your life.

It would also be to your advantage to have the doctor record your weight and have your cholesterol levels on record "before" you begin training. This can be a huge motivational boost for if you have the same measurements and tests done a year later and the improvements are spectacular as I'm sure they will be. It happens all the time and will be another reward for the effort you have put into improving your health and well-being.

DISCUSS IT WITH YOUR FAMILY: It's important to discuss your triathlon plans with those who are closest to you. This is especially true if you are married with younger children. The time you have for your social life and for your family will be a bit more limited if you plan to devote your efforts to a structured training regimen.

It's also important because should you decide to go on a different, far healthier diet, the food you buy, prepare, and eat might be far different from what your family has become accustomed to.

Initially, beginning a triathlon career can be a bit expensive. This varies of course on just how far you plan on taking your career and the quality of equipment you choose to use. I will discuss that more in later sections.

There is also the cost of entry fees and traveling to and from races to consider. Regardless, if money is an issue, it's best to talk about it in the very beginning so there are no surprises later on.

TALK TO YOUR BOSS: If you are employed, then it can ultimately be very helpful if your boss or company is aware of your triathlon plans. There might be times when you need an extra half hour at lunch for a swim work-out or perhaps you will need time off for a race. By keeping them in the loop, it's more likely they will be more apt to be flexible with your work schedule should the need arise down the road.

Always keep in mind that the people closest to you, whether they are family, friends, or co-workers, might well be on the sidelines cheering for you one day when you are in the last 100 meters of your race. It's very important to keep them involved in your triathlon plans, as they will most likely be your support system in the days ahead.

8. TRIATHLON EQUIPMENT

The triathlon equipment you need will vary depending on several factors. First of all, if money is no object, then you can get the best equipment and tri gear available. On the other hand, if money *is* an issue, there are many ways to cut corners.

Swim Equipment (pros and cons):

Your triathlon swim equipment choices include some items that are optional and some that are essential for your training and/or race day.

PULL BUOYS: These are Styrofoam floats that are designed to keep a swimmer's legs higher in the water to prevent them from sinking too low and causing added drag. Early in my triathlon career I was like most rookie swimmers and my legs would sink way too low in the water.

I assumed I needed pull buoys to keep my feet up and my body in a more or less stream-lined position. Of course this is what pull-buoys did for me, but they also gave me a false sense of security and put added stress on my arms and shoulders. If at all possible, I would avoid using these as they prevent you from learning proper body positioning in the water.

HAND PADDLES: Quite often hand paddles are used in combination with pull buoys. Using pull buoys and hand paddles together really puts added stress on the arms and shoulders. One year I was using this combination far too often and it caused a shoulder injury and I missed 2 weeks of training in the pool. Be very careful if you decide to incorporate pull buoys or hand paddles in your swim training.

KICK BOARD: I just dreaded this piece of swim equipment. Even on a good day it took about 5 minutes to kick my way across just one length in the pool, and sometimes I would actually go backwards or simply not move at all. People were always passing me and giving me this "I feel real sorry for you" look. It was several years before I realized that all that kicking does a triathlete little good by the time the race comes around.

If you learn to swim with proper form, an easy flutter kick is all that is really needed to help maintain proper body-positioning. Over-kicking wears out muscles that you are going to need for the bike and the run that follow. For the pros, kicking might provide extra propulsion, but for the majority of triathletes over-kicking can actually do more harm than good.

SWIM FINS: These can be useful when used at the proper time. When I was really concentrating on a particular drill – which sometimes meant swimming in a slow forward speed – I would use swim fins to help maintain my forward momentum so I could get the most out of the drill.

I have tried all of this swim equipment and would suggest you don't use any of them except for maybe swim fins when working on your stroke. Learn the proper balance and buoyancy without any swimming aids and you will be far better off. Of course if you choose to be part of a masters swim group or have a coach who likes to use all of these aids, then it's best to go with the program or else there's not much point being in it in the first place. It's not my intention to undermine any coach you might have, but rather to pass on my own experience with this equipment. Ultimately, of course, the decision is yours, but it's still best to know of the possible downsides of the training equipment you might choose to use.

SWIM SUITS: Cheap swimsuits are the order of the day. Don't make the mistake of spending big money on them. On average I went through about four pair in a training year. If you are pool training (and probably most of you are or will be) chlorine makes no distinction between expensive and cheap swimsuits, and eats them all equally.

SWIM GOGGLES: It would be wise to try several different types of swim goggles. Everyone has a different facial bone structure and goggles that are great for someone else might leak for you. Also I would suggest buying tinted goggles in case of direct sun or reflection that can be very irritating on race day in the event your swim takes place in the open water as opposed to a pool. If it happens that the water you will be swimming in is murky, you might be better off with a pair of clear goggles. It doesn't hurt to have more than one pair of swim goggles that fit you well and don't leak. If you had a clear pair and a tinted pair, you could decide which ones to wear on race morning once you see what the weather and water conditions will be like for the swim. For example, if it's overcast you wouldn't necessarily need tinted goggles. Just be sure that you have done some swim-training with any goggles you might use on race-day to ensure they fit you properly.

LENS ANTI-FOG: Just to be safe, I always used anti-fog on race day. It can't hurt to be cautious. Use it on race morning to *guarantee* you won't have fogging problems out in the open water even if the goggles are supposed to be fog-free. As a last resort you can also use a thin coating of "baby" shampoo on the inside of the lenses if there is no anti-fog to be found.

WETSUIT: Unless you plan on racing in the tropics or doing only triathlons that involve pool swimming, you will eventually need a wetsuit. It's actually to your advantage anyway as wetsuits provide more buoyancy and will normally make you faster. However their main function is to keep you warm. In most triathlons involving open water swims wetsuits are compulsory, but are not allowed if the swim is in a pool, as it provides an unfair advantage.

That doesn't mean you can't try a wetsuit in a pool during your training. It's actually a good way to get used to how it feels to have one on. As a rule, wetsuits do feel a bit tight and constricting out of the water, but are more comfortable "in" the water. So, don't automatically think a wetsuit is too small for you because it feels tight. The best way to make sure your wetsuit fits properly is to have it fitted by an expert as it's a crucial part of your triathlon swim equipment.

Wetsuits can be fairly expensive, but are not a piece of swim equipment that is essential right away if you plan to do triathlons that include pool swims only. It's also possible to rent a wetsuit from some tri shops depending on what area you live in. Be aware however that rental wetsuits are usually limited and will be spoken for as local race dates get closer.

Bike Accessories:

It seems that every year there is different technology that will make a bike lighter and faster. That's great for pros who are looking for ways to shave minutes and even seconds off their bike split. However, for 99.9% of triathletes who are just starting out, there are countless bikes that will do quite nicely and will not require spending tons of money. How light and fast your bike is will have little bearing on how your early triathlons turn out. What will have more impact is your level of fitness and how well you have honed your bike-handling skills.

PROFILE BARS: I don't believe they've invented a triathlon yet that is wind free and you can normally count on the wind blowing in your face at some point on the bike course. Profile bars are great for reducing wind resistance and conserving your energy for the upcoming marathon. If possible, try and have your shift levers mounted at the very front of your profile bars where your hands meet. That way you're not sitting up or reaching down to shift gears. I used something in the early days of triathlon called "swift shifters" and they were great, but today's bike technology is far more advance and there many more options available to you. In the early stages of your triathlon career it might be best to ride without aero-bars until you are more adept at handling a bike without them.

BIKE COMPUTER: Some bike computers have way too many functions. All you need is cadence, speed, and an odometer to tell how far you've gone. That way you're not forever pushing buttons to find the proper setting. Be sure to look at all the different models before choosing one.

CLIPLESS PEDALS AND SHOES TO FIT: Clipless pedals are a great invention. It is one of the key pieces of triathlon equipment that has come along since the days when triathlon was born. Once the tension is set properly, they are easy to get in and out of and allow for a much smoother and more economical pedal stroke than the old toe-clips we used years ago.

Just make sure that the shoes you buy fit into your pedals as there are several models available. It's best to have experts fit your shoe to the pedal as the tension setting is very important. The fit should be tight enough to prevent your shoe from snapping out of the pedal during normal peddling action, but loose enough to enable you to get in and out of them when you have to.

WATER BOTTLE CAGES: There are several places you can have water bottle cages mounted. The normal positioning is on the bike frame just below the seat. Personally I preferred dual water bottle holders that fit behind my seat, and also had two cages mounted on my bike frame. This worked well for long training rides and allowed me to carry plenty of water. Often for an Ironman race I would attach a water bottle between the handle bars, complete with a plastic straw. That way it was possible to just lean forward and take a sip without having to remove the bottle. Nowadays you can get water bottles that are designed for this purpose.

Keep in mind that the more water you carry, the more weight you will pushing down the road. The shorter your triathlon, the less water or drink supplement you will need. You can have several bottle-holders attached, but only use the ones you need for a particular race and leave the others empty. For instance in an Ironman, there's no point in carrying four full water-bottles on your bike during a race if there's an aid station with fresh water bottles at five mile intervals. However, in a long training ride, you will *need* to carry plenty of water.

HELMET: This is a mandatory piece of biking equipment. You can't race without one, so just find one that's comfortable, fits you well, and meets all safety standards. Remember, if it's too loose, it will fall over your eyes when you lean forward into the profile position, and that will drive you crazy. There's also a very good chance that a loose fitting helmet might fail to protect your head properly in the event of an accident. If it's too tight it will be uncomfortable and could give you a headache. The trick is to keep adjusting it until you find the perfect tension.

SUNGLASSES: This is one piece of equipment you *must* have for your triathlon training and racing. Of course it's essential to protect your eyes from the sun and glare, but more importantly, it's necessary to protect your eyes from debris and bugs blowing in the wind. This means wearing sun-glasses whether there is sun or not. I always wore yellow-tinted glasses because they brightened up even the most overcast days.

Run Equipment:

SHOES: Of course well-fitted running shoes are a priority. I've tried every sort of shoe you can imagine over the years, and have come to this conclusion: You can train just as well and stay just as injury free in $75 shoes as you can in $150 dollar shoes. For instance, what if an outlet has a brand new 2008 model shoe on sale for $89, and sells the new, improved (same shoe) 2009 model for $169? It doesn't necessarily mean there is anything wrong with the earlier model, it's just a case of the manufacturer making small changes to their product to in order to keep pace with the competition.

If you find a pair of runners that fit you like a glove and never cause you blisters or sore feet, then you would be wise to put that pair away once they are broken in and save them for race day. I had one pair of shoes that I wore for 6 Ironman races, but never wore in training because I wanted them to last as long as possible. It was like putting on a favorite pair of slippers at the bike-run transition.

It's a big mistake to buy a brand new pair of running shoes just for race day. It's important to spend time breaking them in first. As a matter of fact, all your equipment should be tried and tested in training and not in a race.

FUEL BELT: It can be very irritating to run with a water-bottle strapped to one side of your body. It can often make you feel like you're somehow out of balance. You should really make a fuel-belt part of your triathlon run equipment for training and racing. The belt I prefer holds 6 smaller containers. They are spread out around your waist so you don't feel out of balance and you hardly know they're there during your runs. They are available at most running and triathlon stores.

WEAR A CAP: Wearing a cap is not nearly as important on shorter races or on cool, cloudy days, but I wouldn't be without a cap on those hot runs of 10k or more. A cap will protect your head from the sun, but is also great for pouring water or ice into. This helps to keep your body temperature down. It's important to drink enough in the heat, but it's just as important to keep your head, shoulders, and arms cool and moist in order to keep your body core temperature down.

Talking about equipment might not be the most interesting part of any triathlon book, but it's necessary, as many people have no idea where to start. Also, it's very confusing these days because there is just a huge variety of triathlon gear in today's marketplace.

If you cannot afford a lot, but competing in a triathlon and making positive changes in your life is what's truly important to you, don't be scared off by all the costly equipment, accessories, and clothing that is available today. Don't give up on your dream because you think it's simply too expensive.

We didn't have a lot of choices back in the early 1980's. There really was no triathlon gear available. I lived in Calgary at the time and scoured the city for a pair of tri-shorts to wear in my very first triathlon in Kona and got the strangest looks when I inquired at the local running stores.

It wasn't until three days before the Hawaii Iroman 1984 race that I managed to find goggles that didn't leak and a pair of tri shorts that an American guy was selling out of his hotel room in Kona.

When I learned how to swim for that first race I didn't know about kickboards (thank God) pull buoys, hand paddles, and all the other gadgets that were supposed to make you a better swimmer. I just went back and forth and back and forth in the pool with the worst swim stroke in the history of the world until I could do 2 miles in the pool. That's the stroke I took to my first ever open water swim in Kona 1984.

There were no fancy "skin-tight" cycling and running clothes. There were no profile bars, bike computers, clipless pedals, or titanium. Power bars, gels, and all the other energy food that you supposedly "need" in order to get to the finish line of a triathlon had yet to be invented.

Basically the early triathletes went into their races with nothing more than an overwhelming desire to be part of something special.

It's great that there is so much high-end equipment and cool clothing available for today's triathlete. If you can afford it, go for it. Reward yourself for doing what it takes to better yourself. On the other hand, if you don't have a lot of money available, then go for it anyway. Get a used bike if it's your only option. Just be sure if fits you properly. A $12 pair of sunglasses will protect your eyes from foreign objects just as well as an ultra-cool $250 pair, and you can buy swim suits on special. However, don't skimp on a helmet, bike shoes, or running shoes. You can buy these items on sale and still purchase good functional quality, so take the time to shop around.

There are *tons* of used triathlon equipment available because triathletes are constantly upgrading as their careers progress. You just have to go out and find it. Go to E-bay, check out newspaper classifieds, and ask at local bike shops about any used bikes or great upcoming bike sales. Often they will sell a customer's used bike on consignment if that customer is buying a new bike from them. You might even luck out and find one with all the tri-accessories already on it.

If all else fails, put your own "used tri-gear wanted" ad in the local paper or on the local fitness center bulletin board. It might just save you hundreds of dollars.

My point is, there is always a way. Don't let money be the sole reason that keeps you from realizing your triathlon dream. If it's in your heart and you persist, special things happen. It's just the way it's always been with this amazing sport.

The best example I can give is an incident that happened when I had just arrived at the Kona airport in 1984 to take on the Ironman in Hawaii. I simply can't tell this story enough.

There was a girl standing there with nothing but an old bike with a beat-up helmet tied to the handlebars, plus the worn back-pack that sat on her small shoulders.

She called out "will anyone share a taxi to Kona?"

How cool is that? Here's this twenty-something mere wisp of a girl coming to take on what was the most challenging athletic event in the world at the time, with not much more than her determination and heart.

Sure someone gave her a ride. It wouldn't surprise me if she didn't have a place to stay and slept on the beach or found someone who would share their accommodations.

The one other thing that I will never forget is the fire in her eyes. My God, this girl was on a mission and nothing was going to get in her way.

There is not enough high tech, glitzy, or super-expensive gear in the world to replace the passion and fire that burns somewhere deep inside all of us. It's just that so many people just never let it out.

Don't let yourself be one of them.

Find a way. You will never regret it.

9. MORE ABOUT WETSUITS

I thought I should discuss wetsuits a bit more because most likely they will be something you know very little about if you are completely new to triathlon. Also, they are an important and necessary part of your triathlon gear once you decide to take to the open water.

I can remember being in a triathlon around 1987 and it was a 1.2 mile swim in the coldest water I have ever been in. As far as I can remember, there was not one person with a full wet-suit on. There were some of the early "farmer-john" styles around, but they really did nothing to keep you warm. It took me about 5 tries to get on my bike in transition because I was so cold from the swim.

It was a few years later when the full wetsuit became available and soon sleek wetsuits with names like Quintanaroo and Orca were all the rage. As a matter of fact, I still have an Orca Predator wetsuit hanging in my closet. Now you will also find names like Zoot, Nineteen, 2XU and Aqua Sphere and many others in the retail market-place.

There are several key things to keep in mind when selecting your wetsuit.

A TIGHT FIT: It's essential for a wetsuit to fit tightly, otherwise water will collect in any areas where the suit sags. This will not only slow you down out in the open water, but more importantly, it will cause you to waste energy you can't afford to lose. One of the main features of a wetsuit is to keep you more buoyant and stream-lined. It defeats the purpose if the wetsuit is too big for you.

The very first time you put a wetsuit on, you will no doubt wonder how the Hell you are supposed to swim in it.

If it feels so tight that you think your nose is going to bleed, then you pretty well have a perfect fit, however if the veins on your forehead pop out it may be a touch too tight. It will take some getting used to, but in time you will become more comfortable with the tight fit of your new wetsuit.

SIZING: There's no guarantee that every manufacturer will have the same sizing guidelines, so with that in mind all sizes may not be equal. Always use your body weight as the main indicator when selecting a size from any of the wetsuit brands. For instance if they have a chart that makes you a small according to your height, and a medium according to your weight, always go with the size according to weight. In this case, a medium would most likely be the best choice.

Putting On Your Wetsuit:

- Use a lubricant like body-glide around your neck, wrists, or ankles or anywhere else you think the wet suit will get hung up.

- If you wear socks while putting your wetsuit on, it will make it easier to push your foot through the leg of the wetsuit. You can even use a plastic grocery bag. Just make sure you get rid of the socks or bag before the swim starts or you may get some odd looks. Actually, let me rephrase that. You *will* get some odd looks.

- Always work from the bottom to the top when putting on your wetsuit. Pull it snug a bit at a time as it's too late to tighten up your ankle area once you are pulling the wetsuit over your shoulders. Basically, you would have to start all over again.

- Be sure that the suit is tight in the crotch area. That's the way it's supposed to fit, and if it's not tight in the crotch area, then you will struggle to get the wetsuit on over your shoulders.

- Once the wetsuit is on and zipped up, you can lean forward and pull up any material that may have bunched around your stomach. This will make your upper body feel much more comfortable and less restricted.

- Take your time and get it right, because it will make for a much more enjoyable swimming experience.

Don't wait until the swim start of your triathlon to try out your wetsuit for the first time. Try it out in a pool, or better yet, go out with some friends and try it out in the open water. Regardless, be sure to try it out so you can get used to how it feels.

As uncomfortable as a wetsuit might feel when you first put one on, you will be pleasantly surprised at how much better it feels once you are in the water. Your wetsuit will provide more buoyancy, and at the same time it will help keep your body in a much better swimming position.

10. WHAT TO WEAR ON RACE DAY

During training, you pretty well have to dress for the weather in your part of the world. For instance, I was used to running in cold weather and wearing as many as four layers of clothing in sub-zero temperatures. The possibility of spring storms meant being prepared with gloves, arm-warmers, jackets and shoe booties depending on the weather forecast on those bike training days.

When it comes to race-day clothing there are several options available.

Tri-suits are perfect if you don't want to take the time to make complete clothing changes during transition. They are also ideal if you are in shorter races that do not come with change tents in the transitions area. You simply wear the tri-suit under your wetsuit or during the pool swim and you're good to go for the other two events. They are padded for the bike and it's not necessary to change into bike shorts. Usually they dry out pretty quickly, but you may be cool in the early portion of the bike ride.

A second option is tri-shorts and a separate top. The shorts are padded for the bike and like the tri-suit, you just wear the shorts and top under your wetsuit or just swim in the top and tri-shorts if it's a pool swim.

A third option is to just wear a swim suit (and wetsuit if necessary) and make a complete change into clean and dry cycling clothes. Then make another complete change at transition two into running clothes. In the event there are no change tents, just put on a top and pull your bike shorts on over your swimsuit. This would be a good spot to use tri-shorts as well as the are padded for the bike and light-weight for the run.

In my later races when time was more of a factor for me, I went with the second option. I preferred a separate top, because I had pockets (similar to a cycling jersey) sewn into the top to hold food for the bike portion of the race. Normally tri-suits don't come with pockets and its not really the type of material you can sew a pocket onto. Also, if I felt like changing into running shorts at the second transition, it was a simple operation. Just wear the same top and change shorts.

The clothing you choose will make a difference to your comfort level on race day. I would recommend for your first triathlon, that you take your time and go with clothing option number three. Just wear a swimsuit (and wetsuit if required), make a complete change into cycling clothes, and make a complete change into your favorite running clothes and shoes for the marathon. Taking the time to choose the triathlon run equipment that is perfect for you will make your triathlon much more enjoyable and efficient.

Also be aware of the weather conditions on race day and dress accordingly. A cool, rainy day will mean you might want to wear cycling tights to cover your legs in the bike and most likely you will need a jacket and possibly gloves for the bike and run. Sometimes the bike portion of a triathlon will start out cool as it's early morning, and then warm up considerably as the day wears on. In this case you might consider wearing arm-warmer's on the bike instead of a jacket. If you don't want to buy arm-warmer's then just cut the feet from some long sports socks and you have instant, disposable arm-warmers.

Keep in mind that races like the Ironman provide complete change facilities (tents) for men and women at both transitions. This may not be the case in shorter races. Just make a note of what change facilities will be available for the triathlon you are doing, and choose your race-wear accordingly. Also, you can wear tri-suits, tops and shorts, or just swim suits under a wetsuit if your race calls for an open water swim. In the event that it's a pool swim, its even easier as you don't have to worry about getting the wetsuit off.

Important Accessories:

TRIATHLON WATCH: Actually, it might seem like a flagrant expense to some, but you should have a triathlon watch. Of course the original triathlon watch is the Timex Ironman watch, but there are many other makes out there to have a look at. It all depends on how much you want to spend.

I suppose the Timex Ironman watch has a certain appeal because Timex was a huge sponsor of the early Hawaii Ironman races in Kona. The Timex Ironman watch was born in the heat-drenched lava fields of the King K. highway and in the howling sea winds that still crushes many on the Ironman bike course as they start the long climb to the turn-around at Hawi.

A tri-watch is important for many reasons. It does way more than just keep time for you. First of all, they are waterproof and ideal for timing your swim laps or keeping track of how long your latest 1000 meter swim took you to navigate.

However there is another very important reason to have one of these watches. They have a timer function that enables you to set them to beep at pre-determined intervals.

For instance, I would set the watch to beep every 20 or 25 minutes out on the Ironman bike course. This gave structure to my eating and drinking plan for the ride and was instrumental in ensuring that I ate and drank at regular intervals.

It's quite surprising how quickly time passes and it's easy to lose track of how much you've been drinking and the last time you had a drink once you get caught up in the action that's going on all around you.

Even for shorter triathlons, it's extremely important to pay attention to being properly hydrated. Even if the run is 5k or 10k as opposed to the full marathon distance of the Ironman, the heat of the day can still cause problems for those who forget to drink at regular intervals and keep properly hydrated.

If you are planning on progressing to the Ironman distance, or perhaps have the Ironman in your sights for your next race, it's important to get used to the time element and just exactly how long it takes you to cover certain distances in the swim, bike, and run. Remember that in the Ironman you have three cut-off times to be aware of. If you miss the swim cut-off time or the swim-bike combined cut-off times, you will not be allowed to continue in the race. If you miss the finish line time of 17 hours, you will not be an official finisher.

If you start your watch as soon as the swim start gun sounds you will know exactly how much time has expired as the day progresses. The official race clock never stops, and if you are going to be close to missing a cut-off, a tri- watch will be your best friend as you pace yourself to ensure you get there on time.

Also keep in mind that your watch battery could be running down if you have had your watch for some time. It would be well worth the expense of replacing your old battery with a new one as race day gets closer. The last thing you need is to have your watch quit on you half-way through a race, especially when you are counting on it to time your drinking intervals and your cut-off times.

ID BRACELETS: It doesn't matter if you are training or racing, an I.D. bracelet is always a good idea. Race organizers can always track you using your race number, but it's a good idea to always wear an I.D. bracelet whenever you train or race. Of course it will include your name, address, and contact person, but more importantly it will record any health conditions or allergies that you might have. This is one of the first thing that doctors or emergency personnel will look for in the event you are incapacitated.

11. ABOUT HEART-RATE MONITORS

Taking the time to learn how to use a heart-rate monitor has the potential to enable you to get the most out of your training and races. If a heart monitor is used properly, it will ultimately teach your body to burn fat as opposed to carbohydrates. This will greatly increase endurance because normally athletes run out of gas in around two hours if all they do is burn their stores of glycogen. It goes a long way to explaining why the mystical "wall" shows up where it does on pretty well every marathon course in the world. It's at that point where athletes who push themselves too hard, too soon, run out of gas.

If those same athletes taught their bodies to burn fat stores by training and racing in their "fat-burning zone" they would not hit the wall and would end up having a better result. Ultimately, a heart rate monitor will encourage you to run slower in order to finish faster. It will also make for a much speedier recovery because you will not be pushing your body beyond reasonable limits..

A heart-rate monitor can be an excellent training tool in helping you prepare for your triathlon. In a nutshell, following a heart-rate monitor program teaches your body to work more efficiently. A heart monitor teaches you to be aerobic as opposed to anaerobic.

AEROBIC: Workouts where you are burning fat as your source of energy. A heart-rate monitor helps you accomplish this.

ANAEROBIC: Workouts where you burn only carbohydrates as your source of energy. Proper use of a heart-rate monitor will keep you aerobic and prevent this from happening.

When endurance is paramount, teaching your body to conserve carbohydrates and burn fat is ideal for a very simple reason.

Your body doesn't store a lot of carbohydrates. So during your race, if that's all you burn, you use up your glycogen stores too quickly. Glycogen, simply put, is stored carbohydrates. In a physically demanding event like an Ironman Triathlon or a triathlon of any distance for that matter, once you use up your glycogen stores, you will hit the proverbial wall almost without warning.

A heart monitor will guide you in staying in your ideal fat-burning range. If you are in poor shape to start with, you will be training at a very slow pace at first. If you are patient and ease yourself into your training, you will find that eventually you will be able to train at a faster pace and still stay below your maximum aerobic heart rate. Also, by staying out of the anaerobic zone, your recoveries from training will be much faster and less painful. Better still, your chances of being injured will be diminished.

I trained with a heart-rate monitor for years and had great success. It really did put me more in tune with how my body responded to training, racing, and resting. I would highly recommend giving it a try.

As far as what brand of heart-rate monitor you want, I've always gone with Polar and have never had a problem. They are reliable, and come in a wide variety of models. For instance, you can buy just the basic heart monitor that has just one function. It shows your heart-rate at any given moment once it's turned on. These can normally be purchased for under $100 dollars.

On the other end of the spectrum, you can purchase heart monitors that will interface with your computer. Normally I find just the basic heart monitor is good enough for me. However, one day I borrowed my coach's high end monitor (around $1000) and wore it during a marathon. Every kilometer I hit a button that stored my heart rate and running time at that point. After the race the coach downloaded the info into his computer, and it was really quite amazing.

It actually did a graph of my whole race, showing and recording the rise and fall of my heart-rate during the race. He could tell by looking at the graph every time I slowed down at a water station. These high end models have many, many functions, and if money is no object they can be very interesting to have. However, the basic model is all you really need to teach your body to burn fat and improve your conditioning while at the same time bettering your chances of staying injury free.

It's amazing how a heart-rate monitor can reveal what's going on inside your head as well as in your cardiovascular system. Just try this simple test once you get yourself a heart-rate monitor. Put it on and make a note of your heart-rate. Now close your eyes and imagine yourself struggling to run up a monster hill or in a neck-in-neck sprint to the finish line for all the marbles.

Make it real in your mind and then open your eyes and check your heart-rate. Chances are it has gone up 15 beats or more.

It's no different if you are knee-deep in the water waiting for the starting gun of your triathlon to sound. If you don't make a concerted effort to control your heart-rate, it will begin to spiral upwards with any pre-race anxiety you are feeling at that moment. That's exactly why so many people sprint from the start line of a marathon like they are in a 10k race. All that pent up anxiety and influx of energy that is usually the end result of resting up (tapering) before the big event, is looking for a place to go. If you let your heart-rate monitor be your guide and obey it to the letter, it will not let you over-extend yourself. It will rein you in and *will not* let you join in the early race stampede to oblivion.

If you stick with a workable heart-rate monitor training plan, and use what you learn in your race, I can almost guarantee you will have a much more successful and enjoyable experience than you will if you have no plan at all. Better still, if you are not in the best of shape, a heart-rate monitor will help ease you into training and will reduce the aches and pains and possible injuries that might result from doing too much, too soon.

Learning how to use a heart-rate monitor properly and find the ideal "fat-burning" zone for you need not be difficult. Read on and you will be treated to an amazing story about the power of heart monitor training when it's done properly.

12. TRAINING EFFORTLESSLY FOR IRONMAN

by guest expert Grant Molyneux

Grant is a long-time friend, and just over 25 years ago we embarked on our triathlon careers together. So much has transpired since those heady days, and for both of us triathlon has remained an integral part of our lives in many respects. Grant is one of the finest triathlon coaches in this part of the world, and is also an accomplished author with a goal of completing 100 triathlons. Just recently Grant published his first book, "Effortless Exercise: A Guide to Fitness, Flow States and Inner Awareness". His great book is full of stories like the one he is sharing with all of us on the pages of this book. This story reinforces the benefits of using a heart-rate monitor to your best advantage. – Ray.

I have always maintained that training for Ironman is *easy*, and every time I say that I get strange looks. Let me explain: What I mean is that when training for Ironman you should stay in your comfort zone the majority of the time. That's right; ninety-eight percent of your training should feel effortless. If you're training too hard, you're setting yourself up for failure. Ironman is a long-term journey of aerobic patience – so mantra number one is to "go easy."

Sure, in the last couple months before the race you'll want to pick it up a bit. Perhaps once a week go a bit faster in each sport and/or complete a couple of test races, but the large majority of your training intensity should feel effortlessly easy. A heart rate monitor helps you from getting ahead of yourself and pushing too hard. Let me illustrate my point by telling a real-life story.

I first met Ken McWilliams late in 2002. He had been training for triathlons for a year with a desire to participate in Ironman on a knee that had been surgically reconstructed. In his own words, Ken approached training by "running as fast and as far as I could each time I went out" and based all his training on pace and distance. Everything was done at race pace.

Consequently, he required frequent visits to his doctor as his knee kept swelling, and his doctor told him he would never do Ironman. Ken eventually signed on with me as his coach because he was frustrated and wanted to see if there was a different way to approach this sport. He had heard that I used a different method in training for Ironman based on time and effortlessness. He was interested because his traditional training was only bringing him more pain, and so he committed to following my counter-intuitive guidance.

I told Ken, as I tell all my athletes, your first step in this sport is to chill out, leave your ego behind, strap on a heart rate monitor, and go out and train in your comfort zone. Ken like many others found this type of training "painfully slow!" He said that in the beginning it was hard for him to slow down, but he stuck with it. He started running in the 8 to 9min/km range and would joke that grandmothers routinely passed him on the pathways. In fact, in my effortless program athletes perform a recovery week every third week as they build their volume. I affectionately call this the "stupidly slow week"!

To determine Ken's optimal training pace I used three basic methods fully explained in my book *Effortless Exercise: A Guide to Fitness, Flow States, and Inner Awareness*. But here's a quick lesson.

The first and most important way to set your upper training limit is through your sensation of comfort, balance, and effortlessness. In training for Ironman you want to feel as if you could continue to exercise all day. In other words, you experience no need to stop at any time, that your pace is even, and that you are in balance with your effort. Experiment with a variety of heart rate monitored workouts to see just where *you* are most comfortable. As you exercise, ask yourself two critical questions:

- ◆ Can I repeat this workout right away without any rest?

- Did I feel effortless the whole time I was exercising?

If you answered "yes" to both of these questions and, for the sake of example, you were exercising at an average heart rate of 125 beats per minute, then set your upper limit at 130 bpm for your next workout and don't exceed this. It's as simple as that. Find your comfort zone and set your limit close to the upper range. Be honest and don't overestimate this limit thinking you'll achieve quicker results. The Ironman distance is one sport where going easier, especially in the first 3-5 years of your training, is actually preferable. If you find yourself second guessing a limit you've picked, simply knock 5 beats off and go with that; it's better to be under than over.

The second method to determine the maximum limit for your training is the point at which you lose your ability to breathe comfortably through your nose. When your ventilation is rhythmic and relaxed you are truly in an aerobic flow state. Once your breathing becomes laboured and you start breathing through your mouth, you've become partly anaerobic and are starting to experience exercise induced stress. For Ironman training there is no need to train anaerobically and drive added stress into your body. The training time dedicated to long workouts is enough, so don't overdo the intensity; there's simply no need.

The third way to determine the upper limit for your training is through a simple blood lactate test. Use a blood lactate level of 2mmol/L to set the upper limit of your Ironman training zone. As a coach, I look carefully at these results for the point where the resting values start to increase from the baseline. This point will correspond to the intensity where your body starts to become anaerobic. Also take into consideration the previous two methods. Intuitive data is just as important as the levels of lactate that accumulate because lactate levels can vary day-to-day and session-to-session. If you don't have access to this testing, simply use method one and/or two; you'll discover that you'll be very close to the lactate method should you choose to get tested later.

With this information in hand we determined that Ken's optimal training heart rate was about 145bpm and we set his upper limit at 150bpm with the advice to go over only if he felt great and only very occasionally.

In his first few years he started training comfortably, keeping his heart rate in the 140s and building his volume and his consistency week to week.

After two years of training progressively he built his weekly volume from 5 to 10 hours a week and went on to complete his first Ironman later in 2004 in a time of 14:55. But what was more important to me as his coach was that his knee was feeling much better, so good, in fact, that he never talked about it. Exercising effortlessly had helped to make him healthier even through his Ironman training! This type of flow state training is health promoting; going easy has many wellness benefits beyond performance.

Ken's basic annual plan was to build his training base by progressively increasing his time all the while keeping his heart rate in his zone. In the last 8 weeks before his yearly key race he devoted one workout a week in each sport to going faster - at a pace he called his "race pace." Other than that, all of his workouts were performed aerobically in his specific effortless training zone.

In 2005 he completed his second Ironman in 13:15. In 2006 he decide to add some marathon training to the mix and qualified for Boston on his first attempt, going on to run Boston later that year. You see, his old 8 to 9min/km pace had improved so much that he was now able to run 5:30min/km at his aerobic heart rate of 145bpm, which left him excited to try his hand at a faster marathon.

By 2007 his goal was to qualify for Kona. So that year he trained by adding more time, building his weekly training to over 15 hours a week, with some weeks exceeding 20 hours, all while keeping it effortless in his aerobic zone and staying focused on his training base. The year 2007 brought an 11:42 finish – close but not there yet, so he gave it one more year.

In 2008, after 6 years of consistency, Ken completed his last Ironman in a time of 10:45, a full 4:15 hours faster than his first race. He credits this entire improvement from consistent effortless training.

Now Ken laughs when we talk about weights: he tried them a couple of times and after being sore and injuring his wrist he pitched that idea! So what does Ken tell people when they ask him how he trains? "Your heart monitor is your speedometer, it will tell you when you can speed up and it holds you back when you are having a bad day. Follow it and it will help guide you to the finish line."

He will also tell you to make sure to warm-up and cool-down fully. To this day he still walks for 20 minutes at the start and end of every single run. That's dedication to the process, and his knee has recovered because of his adherence to this protocol. He also swears by the recovery weeks: "Your body needs recovery. These are the "stupidly painful" slow weeks, but they are needed. If you are coming off the couch, start real easy, adjust your zone downwards, and enjoy the process. You'll be amazed at what your body can do, and over time it will transform so much that you'll be marveled at how you have changed."

So there's the training formula in a nutshell – be consistent, build up your training time, and keep it in your comfort zone by using your heart monitor as a tool. Not only will your times get better year after year, but you'll also get much healthier and that's a process worth buying into!

Coach Grant Molyneux's book *Effortless Exercise: A Guide to Fitness, Flow States, and Inner Awareness* is available online at www.vitalize.ca.

13. STRETCHING

I truly believe that stretching is a learned skill, much like we learn how to swim, ride a bike, or lift a weight. It's not always a wise idea to simply emulate what you see others doing.

Many people who are new to the athletic lifestyle are not really sure how to stretch, and simply check out what others are doing over on the stretching mat at the fitness center and follow their lead. Or perhaps they see the speedy club swimmers at the other end of the pool doing all kinds of impossible stretches and try to do the same stretches themselves.

Chances are, the people they are watching have been stretching for years and know how to stretch properly without fear of injury. It's kind of a paradox that we stretch muscles to warm them up for the physical stress to follow in order to prevent injury, yet at the same time we are stretching cold muscles.

I can think of at least two times early in my triathlon career that I injured myself by stretching too forcefully. One of those times left me pretty sore and unable to run for two weeks. That was the last time I ever stretched. I still warmed up my muscles, but did it in a different way.

Instead of stretching before a swim, bike, or run, I would start every training session with 10 or 15 minutes of very slow swimming, biking, or running. In effect I was warming up the muscles that I was preparing to use in training. This made more sense to me and I never had to worry about stretching improperly again.

There are three options that you might consider.

◆   If you have been stretching for years, then good for you. Obviously you know how to stretch properly and do not have to worry about over-stretching and injuring yourself.

- You can learn how to stretch properly from someone who is qualified to teach you. For instance a swim coach, running coach or perhaps a yoga instructor.

- You can do what I did for years and just start out every training session slowly and give your muscles, ligaments, and tendons time to warm up and stretch out a little before stressing them.

Personally, I believe that if you have no idea how to stretch properly, then you should learn from someone who can teach you properly, and at the same time, get in the habit of beginning every single training session slowly, regardless of whether it's a swim, bike, or run.

14. YOGA AND THE ATHLETE

by guest expert Jeff Harshad

I will be the first to admit that I have little knowledge of the practice of yoga, but have always wanted to include it in my books. However, I have made it a practice not to write about anything I do not have at least <u>some</u> experience with. I'm very pleased that Jeff has taken the time to share some of his thoughts on yoga and how it pertains to athletes and how it can create a physical and mental "balance" that will prove beneficial when one is introducing the sport of triathlon into their life. It seems fitting that Jeff is writing on this topic, as he was actually one of the trail-blazers in the earliest days of the sport. Jeff has also worked with professional athletes including pro hockey player Jerome Iginla. Thanks so much, Jeff, for sharing your thoughts and expertise with us. – Ray.

It was a hot summer night in 1981 when I prepared for my first triathlon, a Bud Light/Timex race in Virginia Beach, Virginia. Sitting at the pre- race (pasta!) meal that night, the race director spoke to us and poked a little fun. "We have 3 groups here this weekend," he began. "This group over here, the contenders who are in it to win; then we have the majority of you, the competitors who are just trying to do your best and maybe reach a personal record. Then" – looking at me and smiling as if we were buddies – "then we have a group of you, like this guy … survivors, who will be happy just to make it across the finish line!" I resented/resembled that comment! All kidding aside, it was a 1-mile open ocean swim with swells that day. It became very clear early in the day that I was battling my mind and the elements much more than my body. My body was ready but it soon became apparent to me that

65

endurance sports require mental and emotional strength as well.

Fast forward to my fledgling yoga experience in the late 1980's as an athlete with the same no pain-no gain mentality. I began to recognize that I needed something that would balance out the drive that seemed to permeate any physical activity I pursued. I was guided by an excellent teacher to use yoga as an experiment in balance. Not on one foot necessarily, but in finding a level of effort that created a release of tension and stress, rather than pushing and creating more tension and stress. Since then, I have refined the practice and context of yoga for athletes. I hope you find it helpful.

The athlete's approach to yoga may differ from the average yoga student, however there are some similarities that are worth exploring. There are 5 key elements which are especially important to an athlete and to the advancing yoga student as well. First of all, it's important to recognize that there are a variety of yoga styles offered. They range from the very "out there" esoteric practices or to extremely physical practices that are simply an intense workout. Neither of these is inherently wrong, yet they may not be in alignment with the intention of your development as an athlete. I offer this information as a tool to develop clear intention around your developing yoga experience as we want you to receive maximum benefits from your efforts and awareness. Once you have a clear intention and your "tools", you may explore a variety of yoga styles.

The 5 Key Elements:

- Tension versus compression: As noted by Yin Yoga teacher Paul Grilley, each of our joints has a unique structure that is basically genetic in foundation. From that we want to look at our range of motion and stress on the structure of the body, as different as

66

those around us, even the yoga teacher. You basically want to feel the "stretch" in the belly of the muscle (tension), NOT THE JOINT (compression). A bit of stimulation of the joint, naturally, is all right.

- Endorphins versus cortisol: A common experience in yoga is to "try as hard as you can," and this is especially true for athletes. Effort is not a bad thing, but if all you are doing is "stretching as hard as you can," then you are not actually practicing yoga. You actually want to find a level of effort where you can breathe fully and deeply, sending a message to the brain that everything is all right. If you always push the body to the limit you may receive endorphins, but you may also be masking a release of cortisol, the stress hormone in the body. You want to find a level in your yoga practice where you are in a rest/relax response in the body (parasympathetic), not a fight or flight response (sympathetic).

- Connection to Self: Why? As many sports psychologists will attest, your relationship with your mind is a key factor in your advancement to the higher level in sport. You eventually want to have a yoga practice which allows you to look at "how am I with myself?" Do I always compete with others? What is my limit of effort? How hard am I trying? Am I enjoying this? These questions and more can surface in a yoga practice if you are not just on auto pilot. So turn off the auto pilot and get the benefit of exploring your mind's tendencies.

- Yin to begin: Yin is a Taoist word which means; lighter, less than, etc. In your yoga practice you want to enter each pose, even the whole practice itself, a bit slower, a bit easier, and with a little less effort. Once you have established yourself in the practice with a full breath and body awareness, then you may choose to add some intensity, but only when you choose. This is especially true when working with an injury.

- Core stability, flexibility, strength, speed: This is a model you may use to develop your yoga practice. I use sequential development with many of the athletes and individuals who want to understand and deepen their yoga practice. We start with foundation, relation to gravity, and the true core (meaning the intrinsic muscles of the spine). Then we begin to develop flexibility around that core that will allow the hips and shoulders to work more efficiently.

Once that is accomplished, you will be ready to develop strength from that platform. Finally, you may start to add speed to the movement. For instance, like a golfer (Tiger?) hitting a ball out of the rough. When properly developed, core stability, flexibility, strength, and speed will all come together and benefit any athlete, including the new triathlete.

This very brief description of some of key components of a developing practice is meant to be exactly that, brief. For further support you may choose to contact a qualified yoga teacher in your area and ask for more specific instruction in these areas. Once the instructor is made aware of your swimming, biking, and running goals pertaining to triathlon, a yoga instructional program can be developed that is specific to you and your needs. However, with these simple principles you may be ready to explore your current practice of yoga, stretching, or simply body awareness.

Your body is your greatest teacher and coach. Perhaps it is time to let it begin to lead you, and I believe you will notice the benefits. Perhaps even *substantial* benefits for you as an athlete and as a person.

www.trinityyogacenter.com

15. CHIROPRACTIC ADJUSTMENTS

I often have people ask me about whether or not chiropractic adjustments are a good thing when it comes to triathlon. Whenever possible I try and avoid writing about anything I do not have firsthand knowledge with. It's true of my website and it's true of my first three books.

However, I'm happy to say that I had great success with chiropractic adjustments during my 30 years of competitive running and my 20 plus years of triathlon training and racing. About ten years into my triathlon career I began to have neck and back problems. It was actually my family doctor who suggested I visit a chiropractor.

I asked around because I was interested in finding a chiropractor who was used to treating athletes. I was involved with skeleton for several years (the Winter Olympic event where you go head first down the bobsled run) and spent a lot of time at the bobsled track, and it was a bob-sledder who referred me to his chiropractor.

I knew I was in the right place when I saw autographed pictures of bob-sledders, pro hockey players and professional dancers on the doctor's waiting room wall. After a series of X-rays and an hour or so of testing, the chiropractor told me my spine and neck were seriously out of sync. I wasn't really surprised when he told me it was most likely from the pounding my skeletal structure took over years of running, hundreds of laps in the pool turning my head side-to-side over and over again, and mile after mile in the profile position on the bike.

Usually a chiropractor prefers to see a patient for quite a few days in a row in the initial stage of treatment. It was explained to me that this was necessary to ensure that the adjustments "held." That's pretty well exactly what happened and after just a few treatments I felt amazingly better. After a few weeks we set up a program of seeing the doctor twice a week as I trained for an upcoming Ironman in Penticton.

At the time, part of the treatments were paid for by the provincial health plan, so it was not too expensive and was well worth every cent that I had to pay. The doctor kept saying he was my "competitive edge" and he was right. I went into Ironman Canada that year feeling better than I had in years. It turned out to be an amazing result and that day, the swim, bike, and run were all personal bests and even after a 3:34 marathon, I later felt I could have run even faster, but I was simply not used to feeling so good and didn't dare push myself out on the run course. I was sure a great hand would come out of the sky and squash me like a bug on the Ironman highway as I circled Skaha Lake.

It never happened.

There was no doubt that I had those chiropractic treatments combined with a better knowledge of hydrating and eating to thank for my results that day. Initially I just wanted him to make me feel better and make my sore back and neck go away, but he went a step further and took me somewhere I'd never been in my entire career. Those were the days before I wised up to the fact that rest was an extremely important component of training. I suppose in hindsight, had I trained smarter and been a lot easier on my body, I would not have needed all the adjustments.

It only makes sense that if you don't push your body beyond reasonable limits, you should be able to do just fine without a chiropractor, however for many people that realization might have come too late and if that's the case, then chiropractic adjustments might well help get you back on track.

If you do decide to seek out a chiropractor, I believe it makes a big difference if you choose a chiropractor who is "in tune" with how an athlete thinks and how athletes can physically over-stress themselves during training. This way the doctor is in a much better position to advise the athlete on modifications in training methods or possibly training regimens that might be less stressful on the body.

Hopefully you heed the advice that's spread throughout this book about easing into your training and listening to your body. This will virtually eliminate many of the physical problems that I dealt with over the course of my career from years of over-stressing my body.

16. WHAT IS VISUALIZATION?

Visualization is what an Olympic high jumper does before he starts his run. He goes over what he is about to do in his mind, and it reinforces the coming effort and somehow imprints itself into his muscle memory.

It's been proven over and over again that visualization is a valuable training tool, and as a result, it has been used by pro athletes and Olympians for decades.

There was a comprehensive test done years ago with high school basketball players. They were divided into three groups. One group spent an hour practicing free throws over and over again, one group did nothing, and the last group all found a quiet place and *visualized* or *imagined* themselves taking free throws for an hour. They imagined holding the ball, releasing it, and watching it fall through the netting.

The group that did nothing had the worst free throw results. The team that practiced did far better, and the group that visualized taking free throws did as well as the group that had practiced taking shots.

So how do you make use of visualization as a triathlete?

Well, say you have a bike ride scheduled but it's pouring rain, and you decide to adjust your training schedule and take the day off instead. Find a quiet place, close your eyes, and focus on riding your bike. Imagine yourself making perfect circles as you spin the pedals. Then imagine hearing the tires humming and the feel of the wind rushing past your face as you cycle in a nice, smooth circular pattern.

Or perhaps you are swimming and using long, smooth, perfect strokes and you're hardly making any waves and your breathing is smooth and calm. Do it over and over and reinforce that image in your mind and in your muscle memory.

When visualization is done properly, it can be a very moving and emotional experience at times.

Perhaps you are training for your very first triathlon. Imagine yourself getting off the bike and beginning your run. You've already done so much that you perhaps thought was far beyond your ability. Maybe the swim worried you, but now the swim and the bike are behind you and it's clear sailing ahead.

Then imagine yourself just a few hundred meters from the finish line. Suddenly you realize how far you've come and as you cross the line you have a revelation that somehow your life has changed for the better, forever.

Play that scenario over in your mind in those quiet moments when you are alone, and one day it will come true. Visualizing your goal will give you strength and courage to never give up on yourself or your dream, whatever it happens to be.

17. MASSAGE THERAPY

by guest expert Shelly MacGregor

I really don't have the training or knowledge to inform you about the many benefits of massage therapy. In order to provide you with helpful "on-the-mark" information I invited Shelly to share her knowledge and experience on the subject of massage with all of us. Shelly has written very eloquently and professionally on the topic of massage therapy, and I will be eternally grateful. She has provided important information for you, the reader, and has opened my eyes as well to the many benefits of massage therapy when it comes to athletic performance and recovery.

– Ray.

As you train your body and expect it to keep up with your mental demands and goals, you will notice areas of muscle imbalance, possible repetitive strains and conditions of tightness or tenderness. This is all a normal response as you start to build endurance and strengthen your body.

Many amateur and professional athletes seek massage therapy during their months of training, days before the race, race day and post race. They have discovered the many benefits that massage can have on their long term health and performance.

Massage specific to your needs as you train for your triathlon:

TRAINING MASSAGE: Used regularly during training, sports conditioning massage can improve flexibility as well as take care of muscle problems before they impair performance. Sport or specific massage techniques help to prevent injury and reduce recovery time from many sports related injuries. During this treatment, therapists are able to give a deeper massage, such as stripping or cross fiber friction. It is also important to do broad effleurage strokes over the area to prevent the muscle from stiffening after the deeper work. However it is necessary to ask the athlete about training in the subsequent days. If they have a rest day the next day, it is possible to work deeper on the knots and trigger points as they have time to recover and rest. Nonetheless, therapists must ask the athlete their schedule, as although there might not be a critical competition coming up, there could be a time trial, which is often just as important as a race or competition. Knowing these details will help the athlete recover quicker and enable them to get back to training. It is important to realize as an athlete, you are working with a professional that has the education to help your performance.

1-3 DAYS PRE-RACE MASSAGE: Massage is an important part of serious training, and can do wonders for sore muscles a week before a big race. Be sure to consult an educated massage therapist; they should be familiar with working on athletes and should know that during this massage, they should not work too deeply. Should this occur, it is possible for the area to become overworked causing the athlete to be sore. For obvious reasons, the athlete must be in the most limber and pain free condition possible. Pre-event massages are largely effleurage, which stimulates circulation. Pre-event massages also calm the nerves of the athlete, as even seasoned athletes feel apprehension before competitions. It is also essential for athletes, as it reduces the chances of injury. Massage increases flexibility and range of motion that in turn helps athletes in their respective sports.

PRE-EVENT: The day of your race, you may want to consider a 10-15 minute pre-event massage. This technique warms up muscles and tendons through the use of invigorating techniques in preparation for intensive use.

POST-EVENT: After cooling down, enjoy a 15 – 60 minute post event massage. This deep flush of your tissue can help relax tight muscles, relieve cramping, decrease muscle soreness and reduce recovery time.

Post-event massages help reduce lactic acid build up as well as reducing soreness. For post-event massage immediately after or same day of the event, therapists have to be careful as muscles are often in spasm. For example, a biker having just finished a race might have spasms in their calves. A technique to help this is compression.

One possibility of administering this is compressing with a closed fist and the proximal knuckles as the contact surface. Another way is to compress the origin and insertion towards one another. Slower effleurage is also helpful for post event treatment as it helps drain other by-products of intense physical activity. Shaking is another technique, and is extremely helpful for athletes whose sports are largely dependent on the strength of their arms and/or legs.

POST-RACE MASSAGE: 4-5 days post your race, see a massage therapist for a treatment that is specific to where you need it most. Tell them how you are feeling, where the tightness is and if you are feeling any pain. Your educated therapist will be able to offer you a treatment that is specific to your needs and aid in your recovery process.

Massage therapy is an important part of everyone's training and lifestyle. The foundation of massage and how it aids the body are as follows:

RELIEF: relieves pain, reduces tension and sedates nerves from firing into an area of great tightness.

CORRECTION: deeper massage with a specific focus on the underlying cause of restricted movement, pain and soreness.

STENGTHENING: massage treatment increases blood flow to areas of injury, allowing the body to heal its self quicker and aid in the recovery of damaged problem areas.

MAINTENANCE: regular massage improves circulation, muscle tone, increases flexibility and reduces risk of injury, maintaining the final stage of healing and prevention.

Shelly MacGregor

Director,

Apex Massage Therapy Ltd.

Calgary, AB

(403) 270-7788

18. TRAINING – WHERE DO I BEGIN?

First of all, there is no cookie-cutter training program for everyone – at least, there shouldn't be.

The sport of triathlon is far too complex, with its three disciplines, to assume that anyone can tell you how you should begin to train without knowing quite a lot about you first, as every person is complex and unique in their own way.

There are two main considerations.

Your Life Circumstances:

A lot depends on your circumstances at the moment you pick out a triathlon somewhere down the road that you plan on entering. Are you seriously overweight, do you smoke, do you drink a lot, have a crappy diet, feel depressed, or perhaps you are materially wealthy and successful but oddly unfulfilled? Do you have low self-esteem, or have you pretty much abused your body and spirit to the point that you *have* to do something positive to turn things around or else your fast train to oblivion will just continue picking up speed and the track of life is beginning to run out?

Well good, we have a starting point. Most likely fifty percent of adult North Americans can check off a few items on that list, and some perhaps many of them.

It doesn't really matter. It's all just fluff and little stumbling blocks of life put in front of us to test our ability to cope and overcome. At least that's the way I see it. We have the option of sinking into an abyss of self-pity, resignation, and hopelessness, or we can do something about the direction our lives have taken to this point.

Every single day we have the opportunity to open a different door and begin a journey that will change the course of our lives for the better, forever.

So, where does your training begin?

It already has.

The moment you picked up this book your training started. The fact that you have reached this point in this book indicates to me that just the idea of becoming so much more is compelling to you.

Triathlon training is not all about swimming, biking, and running. It's about much more, and therein lies the secret and the essence of the popularity of triathlon on a world level. Triathlon is about ordinary people doing extraordinary things. It's about breaking down barriers and realizing we all have the power within to change, to succeed, and bust through seemingly immovable physical, mental, and emotional barriers that have been in our way for years.

All that's needed is for someone or something to open our eyes and give us a gentle nudge or perhaps a BIG FREAKING PUSH in the right direction.

For me it happened one day when I was working on perfecting my beer drinking, smoking, and crappy diet skills. I was on the fast track to nowhere and in the "prime" of my life in my late twenties. It was 1976 and as usual I was laying on the couch drinking beer and channel surfing when I came across the final 5 minutes of the Olympic marathon. I was mesmerized watching the leader come into Olympic Stadium all by himself in front of over 60,000 spectators.

For some reason it flicked a switch and a light inside me that was fading and flickering burst into a bright burning flame and I thought, "Wow! It would be so great to be like that guy and be just seconds away from finishing a marathon. At the time, the marathon was the ultimate endurance event in the world.

In a few short moments I went from wondering "how great it would be to do it" to "maybe I could do it" to, "I'm going to do it!"

THAT WAS THE MOMENT MY TRAINING BEGAN.

The beginning is the moment when you realize with a clarity that you are going to do it! The moment you commit to taking your life in a new direction, and there is no more "should I, can I, or will I". There is just an acceptance that the time for you to make a change has come.

Taking that first step was the hardest for me and most likely will be for you, but from that moment on you are reborn!

I went from that instant in time on the couch to the finish line of my first marathon in 8 months. It was a marathon that I did in 3 hours and 28 minutes and my life was changed forever. That one revelation, that one much needed "kick in the pants" has brought me to where I am today, writing this book for you.

Yes, your training has begun.

Your Athletic Ability:

So what do you know about swimming, biking and running? I have yet to meet a triathlete that had to learn how to ride a bike from scratch in order to do a triathlon. I'm sure they are out there somewhere, but I have never met one. Most of us learned how to ride a bike when we were children. In triathlon, all you are doing is getting on a faster, lighter, more agile bike, but at least you have a starting point. Chances are you even have a mountain bike leaning against the wall in the garage.

Are you one of the fortunate ones who already knows how to swim and you are at ease in water over your head? Good for you! However, swimming might be completely new to you and it will be necessary to allow for the time it will take to reach a skill level that will give you the confidence to finish the swim comfortably in any triathlon you have decided to enter. Has it been years since you ran more than 30 meters? Does it seem far beyond your ability? Sure it might feel that way now, but give it time.

As I mentioned earlier, one of the first things you should do is *pick a race* that is going to be your goal to focus on. Allow yourself the necessary time to train, learn, and adapt to the new challenges your triathlon will present. The more you have to learn and the more you have to do to prepare your body, the further away your race should be. Your race could be a few months away, or a few years away. It doesn't really matter. What's really important is that you are beginning the journey to your day of destiny.

For instance once I decided to take on the Hawaii Ironman, I had to allow an extra year just so I could lose my fear of the water and learn how to swim from the beginning. I also had to learn all about road bikes. I could run, so it seemed logical to spend the bulk of my training time working on the disciplines I didn't know much about.

82

Just for an example, say your race is one year away..

For the first month or so you will be busy doing things like visiting your doctor (I hope!) picking out your triathlon gear and bike, finding a swim coach, joining a yoga class, or perhaps finding the perfect diet that will enhance your training and physical transformation.

I believe your key focus word for the first four or five months should be "technique."

Don't worry about how fast you are going, and concentrate more on how you are getting there. If you already know how to swim, work on developing a long, smooth, relaxed front crawl that is perfect for any triathlon. If you don't know how to swim, then get a coach and learn how, and then work on developing the same long, smooth, relaxed stroke. Remember, it's not how fast you get to the other end of the pool, but *how* you get there that is the most important consideration in the beginning.

The key element to becoming successful on your bike is learning how to "spin." Basically, you find a comfortable gear and rpm that you can easily handle without tiring. For the early months of your foray into cycling you should seldom if ever be on the big chain ring in the front. An inexpensive bike will tell you what your rpms are at any given time. It seems like the zone that most triathletes like to stay in is between 80 or 90 rpms. I used to do most of the flat sections of an Ironman course at about 85 rpms. Of course that changes on very steep uphills and downhills. The key is to "spin" for the majority of your time on the bike, regardless of how long the race is. As you improve your technique and gain strength, you will be able to "spin" in a bigger gear and as a result, go faster.

In the early months of your training consider "spin" wind-trainer classes or cycling with an experienced cyclist in order to learn what spinning is all about.

You might consider finding a tri-coach who can help you with everything you need to know in order to take on your first triathlon. It may be a more expensive option, but it might be worthwhile to at least make use of a coach's knowledge and expertise long enough to get you pointed in the right direction. Some coaches will have group training sessions, and this might be an option if you would like to enhance your social life while you are developing your triathlon skills.

Develop a sound training diet as soon as possible. It's counter-productive to train your heart out and then ignore the importance of consuming the proper nutrients your body will require in order to begin to rebuild your old muscle tissue with new.

In the first few months, give yourself plenty of rest time. A good starting point is to spend 3 or 4 days a week easing yourself into your training and resting for 3 or 4 days. The amount of days you train and rest will depend on your fitness level when you begin your actual physical training. Try to put the rest days *in between* the work-out days as much as possible.

Four or five months later, when you have learned a lot about proper technique you can begin to add a little more distance to your training and perhaps train 4 or 5 days a week and rest for two or 3. If you decide to train 5 days per week, one of the days might be an easier day. For instance, an easy, relaxed swim. Sometimes this is called "active rest".

So there you have a few starting points for your training. As I said, just reading this book is part of your training. I am sharing many things that I have learned over 25 years of my hit and miss experience with triathlon and passing them on to you. I have invited guest experts because we can all learn from each other and the knowledge these people are sharing with you is priceless.

Training for a triathlon is about learning, understanding, and improving on many different levels as much as it is about being in the water, on your bike, or heading out for an early morning run.

Do you feel it? Do you feel the stirring deep inside of something special about to happen in your life?

Yes indeed, it has already begun. Carpe Diem, Carpe Diem.

19. I CAN'T SWIM A STROKE

I have lost track of how many people who have told me they could never do a triathlon because they don't know how to swim. Many people have it in their heads that if they have gone 30 or 40 or 50 years without learning how to swim that it's never going to happen, and it's simply too late to learn.

Of course it's not too late. It's not a walk in the park learning how to swim as an adult, but neither was learning how to use this freaking computer at 55 years old. All things are possible if you keep your eyes on the prize that awaits once you push all the obstacles aside.

When I was 34 years old and learning how to swim from zero, I wasn't thinking about making it out of the water in the Hawaii Ironman. I was thinking about crossing the finish line. I had that image imprinted on my mind for two years and it sustained me and inspired me though lap after lap of my crappy, inefficient swim stroke. I was about as far from a swimmer as you could possibly imagine, but one day I did two miles in that pool and just knew I was going to be an Ironman very, very soon.

If your focus is on your ultimate goal and you don't waver, you WILL overcome every obstacle in your way. Sure it's hard to learn how to swim if you are an adult and have never swum a full length in the pool, let alone been out in the open water. It's even harder if you are not fit and are actually fighting a battle on two fronts.

I will tell you a lot of things in this book, but I will never tell you it's easy, and I will never tell you that you can't.

What truly great accomplishment is ever easy? The very essence of triathlon is that it compels you to become more than you ever thought you were capable of. Even at this very moment I still get goosebumps thinking about crossing the finish line in Kona, and that was 25 years ago. Was it worth the effort it took for me to learn how to swim? You bet it was and it will be for you as well when you achieve your ultimate goal.

The good news is, there is a swim technique that will make learning to swim from square one, or perhaps improving your current swim stroke, much easier than you ever thought possible.

20. SWIM SMARTER, NOT HARDER

by guest expert Terry Laughlin

There's no need to let your inability to swim prevent you from becoming a triathlete. Terry has enabled many people around the world to learn how to swim and realize their triathlon dreams through his Total Immersion swim concept. I don't believe I've ever seen a nervous, uptight fish, yet in my early triathlon years I was seldom relaxed when I swam. Thanks to Terry and the Total Immersion concept, I learned how to relax in the water and actually began to look forward to the swim leg of the triathlon for the first time. With this new change in technique and attitude I found that my swimming not only became easier, it also kept me so relaxed that my heart rate stayed at low levels and allowed me to conserve energy for the bike and the run. – Ray

Earlier this year I watched 3200 neoprene-clad bodies churn up the murky waters of Lake Pontchartrain during the New Orleans 70.3 Triathlon, Two weeks later, 4500 athletes swam 1500 meters in Tampa Bay at the St. Anthony's Triathlon. Race directors estimated that about a quarter of them were new triathletes. In other words, in just two races some 1200 novices plunged into a distance swim in open water, surrounded by thousands of others, arms and legs churning, and water boiling from the ruckus.

Is there a more daunting athletic challenge than for a relatively inexperienced swimmer to traverse a mile or more of open water . . . in crowd conditions that – to a novice – seem chaotic . . . without lines to guide them or a wall to rest on . . . before cycling and running up to 138 miles? Beyond what they face in the race itself, new triathletes face two significant challenges: One, humans really aren't meant to be swimmers. Two, making sense of the flood of often-conflicting advice on how to solve the first challenge.

In 20 years since founding Total Immersion, I've met, observed or coached thousands of triathletes, and seen the various ways in which they approach swimming. They range from the somewhat fatalistic: "I'll tough it out" or "I can survive it with my wetsuit" to thoughtful and patient – carefully planned, long-term self-improvement projects focused on pursuit of swimming mastery.

All start out seeking to answer the same question: "How can I swim faster?" The answers they arrive at are as different as their approach, ranging from simplistic (Move your arms and legs faster) to nuanced and analytical. I'm writing to recommend the latter path by citing some empirical evidence about swimming that should become part of the store of essential knowledge among new triathletes. Let's start by clarifying your objective: I suggest you set two goals for your first, or next, triathlon swim:

◆ To jog out of the water and be pleasantly surprised by your time, due to how effortlessly you achieved it; and

◆ To have your experience during the swim be so positive that you eagerly anticipate your next one. Here are three ideas that can help make that a reality.

Keep your powder dry:

This proverb, attributed to Oliver Cromwell, means "Act only when action will be effective." Apply it in a triathlon by being mindful that, as Runner's World editor, former Boston Marathon champion and avid TI swimmer, Amby Burfoot has written, "It takes only a little more energy to run a little faster; it takes a lot more energy to swim a little faster."

In more specific terms, physiologists estimate that a 10 percent increase in effort will roughly translate into the following increase in speed in the three disciplines: Running - 10 percent, Cycling - 6 percent (because of wind resistance); Swimming - 3 percent. If you apply those figures to the approximate median splits for the 2008 Hawaii Ironman of 1:25 for swimming, 6:30 for cycling and 5:30 for running, you get the following return on a 10 percent increase in effort:

Swimming: 3 minutes

Cycling: 23 minutes

Running: 33 minutes

Takeaway: The next time you're in the water and feel the urge to work a little harder to stay with or pass someone else, let them go. Pass them on land instead.

Better engine on land. Better vessel in the water:

Race outcomes – even race instincts – are determined in training. To make the best use of your investment of scarce energy and time in training for three disciplines, it's essential to know what kind of effort will result in the greatest improvement in performance. According to Mayo Clinic exercise researcher (also a veteran marathon runner and Masters distance swimmer) Dr. Michael Joyner, performance in running and cycling are 70% to 80% determined by fitness, while performance in swimming is 70% to 80% determined by efficiency.

Here's more: When elite athletes have been tested on various common measures of fitness – for instance aerobic power and VO2max (maximal oxygen uptake) – the top scores have all been for land athletes. Elite

91

swimmers have often registered fairly undistinguished measures of aerobic fitness.

The takeaway is that, in triathlon's two "dry land' disciplines, gains in speed will correlate strongly with gains in fitness. In swimming, there's little relationship between your fitness level and your speed. What makes the greatest difference, according to tests conducted on all swimmers at the 1992 Olympics by two USA Swimming scientists, is *active streamlining*. A swimmer's ability to minimize drag while pulling and kicking had the strongest correlation to performance of any measure.

Don't Swim Faster. Hold a Better Pace:

The nearly universal instinct about swimming faster is that it happens by stroking faster. Let's clear that up: Swimming speed is not a measure of how fast your arms are moving. Rather it's a measure of the time it takes for your body to cover a given distance. Several factors are far more influential than how fast your arms are moving. The two that matter most are:

◆ In most triathlons, 80% or more of the field will swim too fast in the first 100 to 200 meters, then spend the next 1300 to 3800 meters slowing down. In any swim lasting over a minute, speed is far more about sustainability than velocity. In fact, if you replace the word "speed" with the phrase "pace-holding ability" for any event above 50 meters, your thoughts and actions will immediately become more effective. To hold a better pace, your first step should be to reduce the effort it takes to swim your current speed. That will help you maintain that pace longer without fatigue. Later focus on increasing your current speed.

◆ In order to move your body forward, the propulsive force you generate must be greater than the resistive force (drag) of the water. To move forward faster, you must increase the difference between propulsive and resistive forces. Increasing propulsive force takes work. Decreasing resistive force does not. This makes the resulting increase in speed sustainable – I.E. you'll be able to hold a stronger pace longer without fatigue. Therefore always focus on reducing drag first.

This chapter is excerpted from Terry Laughlin's just-released e-book, Outside the Box, a TI Program for Success in Open Water. Download a free excerpt at http://www.totalimmersion.net/free-stuff.

Terry has been kind enough to offer a 10% discount on purchases through the total immersion website ... www.totalimmersion.net

Simply go to the store page and type ironstruck (all small letters)into the coupon box.

21. THE PERFECT BIKE FOR *YOU*

by guest expert Kevan MacNaughton

Kevan is a good friend, and I was so lucky to have him in my corner back in 1983 when I began my triathlon career in Kona. I knew nothing about bikes and Kevan was instrumental in getting me through those early days. I can tell from interacting with triathletes in person and on-line that there is a lot of confusion when it comes time to picking out the right triathlon bike. Kevan has done a great job of clearing the muddy waters and I really think his advice should be taken to heart as you begin your triathlon journey. Thanks for your great insight and advice, Kevan, and for your support over the years. – Ray.

I've always had a passion for bikes, and when I became involved in the business side of things, it just so happened that the sport of triathlon was just starting to pick up steam. I had my first glimpse of triathletes in action and just what sort of bikes they were riding when my friend Ray, the author of this book, invited me to come to Kona and see the 1986 Ironman Hawaii up close and personal.

The bikes I saw triathletes riding during that race ranged from the less expensive entry level road bikes to the top of the line full aero position tri-bikes that many of the pros (and even age-groupers) chose to ride. Clipless pedals and aero bars had just started to show up in my bike shop in 1985, and quite a few – but not all – of the triathletes had them. Thinking back, I believe it was during that Ironman race in 1986 when I truly first realized how big this sport was going to become and what a huge market there was going to be for triathlon bikes and accessories.

In all honesty, I have to say that in those early years that I sometimes found it difficult to relate to triathletes. More to the point, it would get pretty frustrating at times. It's become clearer to me over the years exactly why this happened, and much of the reason is the mindset that many triathletes have when it comes to picking out their triathlon bike.

In the quest to have better performances and to bike faster, many triathletes demanded the very best and the most expensive of equipment and were not really open to discussing alternatives that would better suit their ability level. In other words, they often failed to take advantage of the knowledge and expertise that we at the bike shop were willing to share with them when it came to choosing the bike that was more suitable to their ability level.

Would you give a brand new driver a hundred thousand dollar performance sports car to start out with?

Sure, I would gladly sell them the very best and most expensive triathlon bike on the market if that's what they insisted on, but if someone were new to triathlon and biking in general and asked my advice on what they should buy, this is what I would tell them.

First of all, there is a big difference between road bikes and triathlon bikes.

If you have not been on a bike since you were a kid, then it makes little sense to spend a ton of money on a sleek, ultra-light, very expensive triathlon bike with the misguided notion that it will instantly make you a better cyclist and triathlete. It makes more sense to ease yourself into the sport of triathlon and in particular biking, and that includes picking out a bike that will match your level of ability.

Ultra fast performance in the bike is not a substitute for developing good cycling technique. If you are new to cycling there is really only one way develop a smooth cycling technique. Riding, and lots of it, over long slow distances (LSD).

Triathlon bikes are built with that straight ahead, aerodynamic speed profile that doesn't really allow you to bike in a lot of different positions. It is a faster riding position, but triathlon bikes require more skill when it comes to "handling" and manoeuvering in tight spaces and around corners. With a good cycling base you will be faster on an aerodynamic tri-bike, but you have to build on your cycling base before graduation to a tri-specific ride.

There is no substitute for time in the saddle, and I believe a traditional road bike design is the best way to start out and accomplish this. A road bike will perform well in a variety of riding conditions from store sponsored group rides, charity rides, commuting, and of course your specific tri-training. A traditional road style frame simply gives you more opportunity to ride and build base mileage.

I really think that the new triathlete should buy themselves a good quality *road bike* and not worry so much about the aerodynamics offered by the profile bars and lower configuration of the high end triathlon bikes, and concentrate on learning the different hand positions that are available with the traditional "drop" style handlebars and improving their balance, smooth pedaling, and bike-handling skills. Once a certain confidence and comfort level is achieved, *then* I would add profile bars to that same bike.

Most likely, your first few triathlons are not going to be about speed and shaving time by being in the profile position and chances are you will simply just want to take part and simply finish your triathlons without much concern for how fast you are going. If that's the case, why take the leap into triathlon bikes from the very beginning?

It makes more sense to upgrade your bike as your overall bike handling skills improve. In other words, you are not letting technology outpace your ability and as a result making it harder for yourself to learn the basic skills that will make you a competent and confident rider. Sure, I would love to sell you a top-of-the-line, expensive triathlon bike, but if I had my way, I would sell you a road bike first and then a triathlon bike when the time is right and your ability matches the bike.

www.thebikeshop.com

22. BIKING BITS

Well, you've had some great insight into bikes thanks to Kevan, but now you are probably wondering how to get started with your bike training.

LEARN TO SPIN: As I mentioned earlier, the key is to spend the first months or even year of your initial training learning proper technique. When it comes to biking there is no doubt that the "spin" is the key.

It's important to always keep in mind that you will be running once you get off the bike. The less energy you use during the bike leg, the more you will have left for the run. The less stress you put on your back, shoulders, and legs, the smoother and easier you will be able to run.

START OFF IN YOUR COMFORT ZONE: At first you may be a bit timid about heading out onto the open road on your bike. I would suggest using a wind-trainer in your home for starters and then if possible find yourself a spin class you can join. The instructor of a beginner class will lead the group and take you though the gears and explain things like spinning, shifting, and proper positioning on the bike.

THINK CIRCLE: I read once that the key to spinning is to think "circle" as you bike. This is one of the better descriptions I ever came across of the ideal circular pedal-stroke and I used it for years.

Imagine there is an egg under your big toe on the downward part of the pedal stroke and you don't want to press down too hard on your toe because it will break the egg. On the bottom part of the stroke, imagine you are scraping dog crap off your shoe. On the upward part of the stroke imagine that you are trying to pull your heel out of your shoe.

Egg-crap-heel, egg-crap-heel, egg-crap-heel.

After a while I was saying that mantra in my sleep, but it worked. It always made me think circle and my pedal stroke became a whole lot smoother and much more efficient.

DON'T FORGET ABOUT BALANCE: Eventually you will have to get your bike out on the road. It's essential because that's where you will work on perfecting your balance and bike-handling skills. Wind-trainers are great but they don't hone the skills you will need to avoid the pothole up ahead, or navigate the downhill turn that's coming up.

BABY THAT BIKE: It may be just in my mind, but every time I wash my car it seems to run better. A bike is no different. If you keep it shiny, clean, and well-oiled it will absolutely *hum* for you.

There is no feeling like that perfect day on the road when the universe is in perfect balance. You feel great, the scenery is stunning, the sun is shining in an endless blue sky and the warm breeze caresses your face as your bike hums and the spokes and gears sparkle in the sunlight.

LEARN BIKE BASICS: You should never mess around with any of the gear adjusting screws, brakes, or anything else on your bike unless you know exactly what you're doing. Leave it to the professionals at the bike shop. However you can learn how to take your wheels off and on and how to replace a tube. It may be frustrating when you are first learning how to fix a flat, but it's essential and gets easier with practice. You can do it over and over again in the comfort of your own home until you get it right.

A well-maintained bike will perform beautifully for you regardless of the make or model you happen to choose. If you take care of your bike, it will take care of you and get you to where you want to go. Once your bike fits you properly and you put in the time and learn about proper spinning, bike-handling skills, maintenance, and other aspects of biking, you and your bike will become one. You will be in sync and one day you will be amazed at how skillful you have become at riding your bike.

Extra Tips:

- If you go to a building supply store, you can buy a length of foam tubing that is meant to protect pipes. It's perfect for protecting your bike frame if you are using a rack that attaches to the back of your vehicle. Just cut a piece that will protect the part of the frame that rests on the rack. This will prevent any rubbing and prevent paint from being worn off.

- If you are going to be traveling for hours and your bike will be exposed to the elements, it wouldn't hurt to cover the gears and chain with plastic to protect them from dirt, grime, and rain that you might encounter on your trip. It's either that, or give your bike a real good cleaning once you arrive at your destination.

- Blue Dawn dish soap is hands down the best bike chain, gear, and grease cleaner you will ever find. Buy some of this if it's still on the market. It has something in it that really cuts through grease, and no, I don't have a relative who owns a Blue Dawn factory. It just works.

- If you are traveling to a race, always check your bike computer and make sure it works when you arrive. Regardless if you have your bike inside or outside, the sensor might get jostled and move, and the computer might not work until the sensor is repositioned. Don't wait until you're out on the bike course on race day to find out your computer doesn't work.

- Take the plug off one of your handlebars and stick a twenty dollar bill in there. Use a bit of tape to secure it so it won't work itself down into the handlebars where you can't get at it. You never know when it might come in handy on one of your long training rides. You never know when you might run into a friend and decide to stop in the next small town for a bite to eat or perhaps you are on a long ride and didn't bring along enough food. Believe me, it can happen. Several times over the years a few dollars and a country store saved me from a long, hard return trip home.

- Okay ... hands up everyone who thinks you are supposed to wear underwear under your cycling shorts. Wow! I didn't know so many people could be wrong.

  The truth is that cycling shorts (with the chamois built in) are made to be worn without underwear. This prevents having to deal with material binding and causing you problems on your long training rides. Actually it's very comfortable and more sanitary to have clean bike shorts on and nothing else. However, care should be taken to wash your bike shorts frequently. You can wash them quickly in the sink after each ride. It's best to have a couple of pairs so you can wash one pair and wear the other if you happen to be cycling two days in a row. Cycling shorts can take quite some time to drip dry because of the chamois.

- Always have at least two spare tubes and a patch kit with you for those longer training rides. A small pump is helpful as well and can normally get enough air into a tire to get you home, but air cartridges are preferable as they are easy to store and will put 100 psi in your tires very quickly. Be sure to have someone show you how to use these. When you practice changing your tubes at home, you will most likely be using tire levers. Be sure to add a pair of levers and an adjustable wrench (in case a bolt comes loose) as well. Your tubes, tire levers, air cartridges and adjustable wrench will all fit in a small tool kit under your seat.

◆ Often there are bike mini-classes sponsored by bike shops that will walk new cyclists through basic maintenance and tube-changing techniques etc. These are an excellent idea and you should attend one of these classes if you have the opportunity.

Chances are your bike will perform beautifully for you and much of what I mentioned will never be a problem for you, but it doesn't hurt to have the knowledge and ability to handle any situation that might arise. It might not be just for yourself. One day you may be out on a ride and find someone else in trouble and you will be able to help them out. In this day and age you can take a cell phone with you on your rides, but it's best to be self-sufficient if possible. If you have a real emergency, then a cellphone is great to have along.

It's not really the triathlons you enter that you have to worry about. There will be plenty of people around if you have problems. Even in Ironman races there are bike mechanics all over the bike course to help people with flat tires and mechanical problems. It's your training rides where you may have to fend for yourself, because you are more likely to be on your own.

23. WHAT'S A WIND-TRAINER?

This is a dictionary definition of a wind-trainer (sometimes called a "spin" trainer): "A training device consisting of a frame in which a bicycle is fastened for stationary riding."

What this means is that you can put your bike on one of these trainers and park it in front of your T.V. if you want so you can watch your favorite reality show while you do some bike training.

I did a ton of wind-trainer biking in my day. One year I did almost all of my bike training on a wind-trainer for an upcoming Ironman in Idaho. I just got frustrated with all the traffic out on my favorite biking routes. I even had a two-movie wind-trainer workout. I would bike on my wind-trainer for 4 or 5 hours and watch two movies. However, it's not something I would recommend to someone new to biking and triathlon. At the time I had already been involved in 13 Ironman races so had a pretty good idea of my capabilities.

As I mentioned earlier, it's a good idea to bike outside so you can hone your bike-handling skills and work on your balance, cornering, and hill-climbing. You also need to get used to riding in the elements like the heat and wind. That's the one big downfall of being locked into a wind-trainer. Sure, you can talk on the phone, read a book, or watch a movie on your wind-trainer, but you really do need to take it outside eventually to get a grasp of real bike riding.

Wind-trainers, on the other hand, are perfect for the days when you are really short on time, or when it's pouring rain and you just have to get that bike ride in. They are also a good way to ease your way into training on a bike if it's new to you and you are a still a bit shy about riding in public.

You will find a wind-trainer very useful when you are ready to give a bike to run transition a try. There is really no way to describe how you will feel the moment you get off your bike and begin to run. It's really something you have to experience for yourself. In that respect a wind-trainer is ideal. You can bike for 30 or 40 minutes, hop off and put on your running shoes and go for a short run. This is a great way to get used to how that transition will feel when race day arrives.

If you happen to go to "spin" classes what you will find is several rows of these wind-trainers set up and all you have to do is take your bike and lock it into the trainer.

As some triathletes get more competitive and up into the half-Ironman and Ironman distance races, they might decide to get a second bike that they use strictly for wind-training. Some triathletes feel they are "beating up" their high end tri-bikes by using them in wind-trainers. This may be true or not, but for your purposes as a beginner it's best to get used to one bike and ride it inside and outside.

With the new technology these days you can buy CDs that have specific bike courses on them and you can bike while doing the Ironman Canada course in Penticton, for instance.

To my way of thinking a wind-trainer is a very important training tool and you should have one if it's within your budget. You should be able to pick one up on sale for around $200. You will most likely get a better price in the summer months.

Like anything else, there are several models of wind-trainers to choose from in a wide range of prices. Just visit your local bike shop and they

106

will help you pick one out that will suit your needs, or you can take
along a friend who is an experienced cyclist and they can help you pick
one out.

24. RUN-WALK. RUN-WALK. RUN-WALK.

Run-walk. Yes, it's worth repeating.

So many people have told me they could never do an Ironman, a half-Ironman, or an Olympic distance triathlon because they can't run a marathon, a half-marathon, or 10k.

It's a misconception and in reality most novice Ironmen run-walk the marathon. As a matter of fact it's a great alternative for a triathlon of any distance.

Of course it's very possible to run the full distance of any triathlon course, but it takes time to get yourself there. Pros do it all the time and so do many experienced age-group triathletes. However it's asking a lot of yourself to expect to go out and do it if you are new to the sport and athletics in general.

Like many new triathletes, I was a runner before I ventured into the world of triathlon. At first I had an illusion of hoping off that bike and powering through the marathon.

Not so fast mister....

Boy, was I in for a rude awakening. This was especially true when your first triathlon is the Hawaii Ironman. In those early Kona races the bike transition was at the bottom of this short, steep hill. Some of us called it "the pit." If the bike transition was at the bottom of the hill, that meant your first kilometer of the run was straight uphill in order to get out of "the pit." I came flying down that hill on my bike (well, because it was downhill not because I was a great cyclist) and this pair of cute Hawaiian girls who were part of the volunteer corp were there to grab my bike when I came to a stop. I was going to show them a *real* runner in action. I took two steps and pretty much every muscle in my body seized up.

I hobbled to the bottom of that hill and went up about 10 feet and wanted to shout ... BRING THE ROPES! QUICK! I knew then that it was going to be a long, hard day out on the torrid lava fields of the King K. highway. I had done pretty well everything wrong.

First of all, I didn't bike nearly enough in my training. My longest training ride was around 40k. I did virtually no transition training, so in reality I had no idea how it was going to feel to run after being on a bike for over 7 hours. I didn't drink drink nearly enough out on the bike and 1984 turned out to be one of the hottest Ironman races in history. I also used way too many big gears during the bike. All of these components are a major factors in how the run portion of triathlon will unfold.

Many of us in those early days of the Ironman really never knew any better and we were basically learning on the fly.

It took me six attempts at the Ironman before I finally ran the entire marathon from start to finish. It simply takes time to get used to switching your muscles over from biking to running in a heart-beat. There are just so many things to factor in that can have a profound effect on how you are going to feel when you get off that bike.

If you can focus on these three suggestions, I'm quite certain you will have a better chance of having a more enjoyable and successful run portion of your triathlon, regardless of the distance of the race.

- ◆ Learn how to "spin" in a comfortable gear and avoid pushing big gears and over-taxing your muscles and burning energy needlessly.

- Be sure to have a proper hydration and nutrition plan in mind leading up to the race and out on the bike course.

- Be sure to practice the bike to run transition in your training on a regular basis. Even if you bike for 30-45 minutes on a wind-trainer, and then run for 15 minutes or so right after; it will help familiarize you with how it's going to feel on race day. As you become fitter and gain endurance, you can lengthen the time of both the bike and run.

Also, when you start getting into a little more distance in your run training, give this run-walk suggestion a try.

Regardless of whether you are new to running or not, always start out with an brisk 10 minute walk to ensure you are properly warmed up. In effect, you are easing your body into the run. Once you are properly warmed up, begin a run-walk sequence for the duration of that run. Everyone's run ability is different, but for sake of this example, run for 12-15 minutes the best you can, and then walk for 2-3 minutes. Repeat this for the duration of your workout.

What you are preparing yourself for is to run the best you can in segments and give yourself a walking break to recover. In other words, you will be going into your triathlon with a sound plan. You won't be like me and many others after me who go into their first triathlon thinking there will be fire coming off the heels of their running shoes. It's not likely going to happen.

This is the plan I suggested for novice ironmen and basically I proposed they train themselves to run or power-walk the best they can between the aid stations and walk through the stations while they recover and take a drink etc. The aid stations are a mile apart in Ironman marathons so it works really well.

There is no reason you can't adopt the same run-walk plan in a triathlon of any length. Just go by your watch as there are not normally aid stations every measured mile in shorter triathlons. So many people prepare for a triathlon with no real plan in mind for dealing with the run and by using this system in training you will have a plan to focus on in your months of preparation. It will also be a relief of sorts to realize you don't *have* to run the entire course.

Of course everyone is different. There are some very experienced runners who make the jump into triathlons and they might be able to run the full distance of the run course in shorter triathlons. There are some of you who will be able to make the run portions longer and the walk portions shorter. There is no "cookie-cutter" format as we are all different and have different levels of fitness and athletic ability. Formulate a plan that works for you and as you get healthier and fitter, you can adjust the run-walk distances. If you are really starting at ground zero, you might be walking *quickly* and then walking slowly to rest and not running at all in the early months.

Say for instance you have 50 or 60 pounds to lose. If you remain committed to your training, regardless if you are running or walking or a combination of both, you *will* improve. This is especially true if you are incorporating a healthier way of eating along with your new, improved athletic lifestyle. As I mentioned earlier, it's not necessarily all about losing weight. It's about getting fitter, and in the process you will eventually end up at the weight that is best for you.

It's always possible to reconfigure the run-walk plan that is right for your ability. Maybe you'll decide to run for 5 minutes and walk for 1. Do whatever works for you, and as you gain fitness and experience, challenge yourself to run more and walk less. It's a natural progression that always give you new goals to shoot for and also makes the sport more enjoyable as you ease yourself into it and increase your fitness and athletic capabilities over time.

Keep in mind that there is no rush. If it takes you 2 or 3 years to get where you want to go and take part in your first triathlon, then so what? The important thing is that every single day of those 2 or 3 years you are making positive steps toward a healthier and happier way of life. You have started your journey and when you begin to witness improvements in how you look and feel it will inspire you and give you wings as you strive for your goal.

25. OVERUSE IT AND LOSE IT

If this is your first foray into the world of triathlon and fitness in general, you are going to be exposing your body to physical challenges that it's simply not used to.

The human body is amazing and will do its best to adapt to the physical demands we make on it. However, you can expect a rebellion of sorts to take place in the early days. It's almost as if every fiber in your body is saying "whoa, not so fast." Well actually, that's exactly what it's probably saying.

That's the whole reason for the concept of warming up and easing into any physical activity and it's even more important if it's a *new* physical challenge for you.

I used to do weight training on and off throughout my triathlon years. It didn't seem to matter how great my overall conditioning was, if I went into the weight room after a long absence the result was always pretty much the same. No matter how light the weights were that I used on the first day, I felt it the next morning when I woke up. It never failed.

My body was always quick to detect something new going on, and yours will be as well.

For many years, I believed that if I persisted, the aches and pains I felt would slowly disappear as my body resigned itself to these new physical demands I was making. Always remember that *YOU* are the boss, and your body will respond to the signals you send. You can have a great diet, a poor diet, be active or a couch-potato, and your body will adapt to your lifestyle whether it's a healthy one or not.

It's not your body's choice. It's *YOUR* choice!

If you train like I did, you can most likely expect to be sore in the early days of your training. Chances are, you will be sore in different areas of your body from the three disciplines. Your leg muscles, knees, ankles, and feet will most likely all act up when you first begin to run. Your back, neck, arms, and shoulders will all be challenged when you bike and swim and your body will be sure to let you know.

The harder you go at your training in the beginning, the more you will suffer through the aches and pains before your body begins to adapt. Even though your body will appear to adapt, there's a good chance you are over-stressing it and setting yourself up for future injuries, and most likely slowing the conditioning progress unnecessarily..

Caution is the keyword to remember when it comes to entering the world of fitness and athletics after a long absence, or perhaps for the very first time. Yes, you can expect to ache and be sore in the beginning if you are too aggressive in your training.. This is not always a bad thing if we use those aches and pains as a wake-up call and ease off. In the early years of my athletic career, I used to think those aches and pains were a good thing and an indication that I was on the right path. It took a lot of years to figure out that I was doing more harm than good and I should have been backing off, not stepping on the throttle.

I would not simply quit training if you become sore. Your body will never adapt if you are continually starting and stopping. Learn from being sore. Learn that you are pushing too hard and back off. Say for example you are very sore from your early running or walking efforts.

Give yourself a rest day and then run or walk some more. Warm up for a good 10 minutes or so by walking easily before you pick up the pace and monitor how your body responds as you begin to challenge it.

In most cases the soreness and aching will dissipate as you repeat the same physical effort that made you sore in the first place, *if* you go easier.

One of the biggest benefits of triathlon is the opportunity you have to ease off on one discipline and concentrate on the others. For instance, if you are out on a training run and feel a sharp pain in your ankle or knee that doesn't seem to want to go away, then take a 3 or 4 day break from running and work on your swimming. There's no impact, and by swimming you will maintain your fitness level.

After your break of several days, do the same run over again, including the warm-up and easing yourself into the actual running. If your legs in general seem to ache a bit, don't worry about it. Often that's pretty well normal and no matter how easy you go at your training, you may feel a little discomfort for a short time. However, if you notice the same sharp pain in the same place then stop running as a precaution and walk back home. You may have a problem that requires medical consultation and at this point I would pay a visit to your doctor.

Your doctor may suggest a longer rest from running or perhaps physiotherapy treatments. Regardless, it is taking a chance if you keep training when you have the same pain in the same place for days on end.

After you gain more and more experience through your training, you will become better at reading your body. You will be able to detect almost right away when something is not quite right. It's really just another great benefit of being fit and active. You just become so "in tune" with yourself and how you should feel.

Often a nagging pain will disappear if you give yourself a rest from stressing the area that hurts. It's when you push and persist despite all the early warnings that you could end up with more serious injuries that will cost you weeks or even months of training.

Most injuries can be avoided in the first place if you ease yourself into your training and don't push yourself beyond reasonable limits. Always keep in mind that triathlons by their nature are *endurance* events. Building that endurance comes over time, and it's not something you can rush. All the training you do increases your endurance slowly, and it's like putting money in a long term bank account. If you put in a little at a time on a regular basis, it grows, collects interest, and will eventually pay off one day in the future.

26. TRAINING, RESTING, AND BURN-OUT

Passion has a funny way of masking logic.

It's not unusual at all for triathletes to have compulsive personalities. I know I do, and what us compulsive types are really doing is making our compulsive tendencies work in our best interests by adopting a way of life that's amazingly beneficial and life-changing in so many ways.

Many of you will go head first into your newfound triathlon lifestyle with a passion. It will be damn the torpedoes and full speed ahead. It's vitally important to learn to temper your drive and passion and achieve a balance between resting and training in order to avoid physical burn-out, sometimes known as over-training.

When I was bitten by the running bug over 30 years ago it really did become my passion. I had no idea how much to run or when to rest. So I just ran until I got tired and in the early days I wasn't a big fan of rest days. I had it in my head that if I stopped running for a day or two, that I would lose all I had gained. There simply were no guidelines to go by and I didn't know any better.

One year I ran for 364 days and took Christmas day off (against my better judgement). At the time, I thought I was having some pretty good race results when I went 2:58 for a marathon and 35:28 for a 10k race. These ended up being my personal bests for years.

Of course my body finally broke down and I think I was one of the very first local athletes to have arthroscopic knee surgery. I believe the doctor who was pioneering the procedure in my part of the country had done a pro football player from the CFL before he operated on my knee.

I still learned nothing from all of that. A week later I was back in training, and within 6 weeks I ran another marathon in a time of 3:08. Arthroscopy is a truly remarkable procedure, and that result even blew the doctor away. Of course he had no idea at the time he was dealing with the running fool from Hell.

Eventually, I had the same medical procedure on the other knee.. The 100 mile running weeks were taking their toll. It was years before I began to learn the importance of incorporating rest into my training.

It speaks absolute volumes to me that in my forties, I set new personal records in both the marathon and 10k races. It made me realize that I had really cheated myself back in the early days. By resting more and training smarter, I actually became faster as I got older. To this day it makes me wonder what I might have accomplished if I knew back then, what I know now.

You can easily prevent this from happening to you. Early in your triathlon career ,take 3 or 4 rest days a week if necessary. If you feel that you just *have* to train more, then make one day an easy one in the pool and work on your long, smooth swim stroke. As you get more experienced and fitter you will most likely be able to get away with 2 or 3 rest days on a fairly regular basis.

If you are getting run-down and feel sluggish, take a weekend off and do something entirely unrelated to triathlon training. Do something with your family. Feeling crappy and forcing your way through training sessions are the early warning signs of burn-out up ahead. When you come back from your rest you'll be surprised at how good you feel and will be eager to get those runners on or get back on your bike.

I believe it's safe to say that the majority of novice triathletes go into their first races over-trained and struggle more than they have to because of not resting enough throughout their training and not giving their bodies that much needed recovery time. Actually, it can go on for years, and unless you begin to realize the importance and power of rest, you will end doing what I did. I cheated myself and pushed my body unnecessarily and eventually paid for it.

Don't let it happen to you.

27. SHOULD I TRAIN ALONE?

Everyone has a different agenda. For some people, triathlon can be a tremendous opportunity to jazz up their social life. What could be better? The people you will meet at your masters swim class, bike spin class, or group running sessions will have the same aspirations and goals as you do. They will know where you're coming from and will be talking your language.

At the same time, there can be a downside to training with others, and eventually you may discover this for yourself. For example, when you swim with groups, you will often find that there are lanes for fast swimmers and lanes for slow swimmers. Usually there is a lane way over by the side of the pool for the *really* slow swimmers. This sort of structure often creates a competitive atmosphere. Many people just don't want to be known as the slowest swimmer, and as a result rush their swim strokes in order to try and go faster and in the process forget all about learning proper technique.

To me, the time to compete is when the starting gun goes off and not when you are trying to learn and improve. If you choose to swim in groups then be aware of this and don't fall into the trap. Ignore what others are doing and listen to the coach and progress at your own speed and eventually you *will* improve and end up being in the next fastest lane.

Keep in mind that you will be trying to balance several things. You will most likely have family and work obligations as well as attempting to become proficient in three different disciplines. In other words, you will not have a lot of time to be waiting around for others who are late for your running date. You have a schedule to keep and it often becomes difficult to fit others into your training schedule.

There is something else to consider as well. Say you plan on meeting up with three or four people to go on a training ride. The chances of you all feeling the same on that day are pretty remote. You may feel like putting the pedal to the metal and the others are poking along, or they might take off down the road and you just want to take it easy but have to push yourself to keep up. Keep in mind that you are on a mission, and must do what's best for you and your training. There is no point in you getting injured because you pushed yourself when you should have been taking it easy.

It's always wise to go on those really long rides with someone else, but make sure you decide before hand what you expect from the ride and have an agreement to either take it easy or pick up the pace. It's much easier to coordinate a ride with one other person than with several people.

There are coaches like Grant Molyneux (a guest writer in this book) who have ideal group training programs that are closely monitored so it's indeed a group session and not everyone for themselves. This is a great way to train with groups, as everyone knows going in what the group dynamic will be because it's structured in a pre-set way. At least that way you know before-hand what to expect and can decide if that group ride fits into your schedule or not.

Always keep in mind that triathlon by its nature is a solitary event. It's also important to get used to being on your own. If you enjoy the social aspects of group training that's great, but make sure that on occasion you give yourself the opportunity to grow accustomed to training on your own and being alone with your thoughts.

Sometimes there is nothing finer than a solitary early morning winter run along your favorite route when ice crystals are sparkling in the air and all you hear is the sound of your measured breathing and your feet meeting the ground in a steady rhythm that speaks of life, health, fitness, and joy.

28. A BIT ABOUT DIET

I won't even attempt to come up with a diet that will suit every new triathlete. It's an impossibility, because everyone has different goals and body chemistry. Some new triathletes have to lose quite a bit of weight, and some may have to bulk up and add muscle.

As I mentioned in an earlier section, carrying some extra weight does not mean you cannot be fit. I was in great shape in the prime of my Ironman career and usually raced at about 148-150 pounds. More times than I can count I would be fighting my way up the endless kilometers of Richter's Pass in Ironman Canada and triathletes (both men and women) who were obviously carrying a lot of extra weight would go spinning right on past me.

Did I think I was getting passed by a fat triathlete? Or did I perhaps think they did not belong?

Of course not. What I thought was "holy crap, that is one strong cyclist."

If you go into triathlon training and combine your new fitness regimen with a sound diet, you can't help but lose some weight, but more importantly a good diet can enhance your endurance. Once you start eliminating the simple carbohydrates from your diet and consume an ideal balance of healthy fats, proteins, and complex carbohydrates you will change your blood chemistry for the better.

Main arteries that have become constricted over years of a sedentary lifestyle will clear up, and the result will be less effort required to move blood to the muscles that are being worked. If you combine that with lungs that are becoming stronger and more efficient through your training, you will start to notice some big changes taking place. The heavy breathing that used to come every time you climbed some stairs, or did anything else physically taxing will soon disappear. You will sleep better, look better, and feel better. You can't really lose if you are always aware of what you are consuming and begin making the smart choices.

Early in my running career I was under the impression that I could eat whatever I wanted because I ran so much and never gained weight. It was true I never gained weight, but all the ice cream and donuts were screwing up my blood sugar and hurting my endurance and overall energy. As good as I felt I was running, I could have done a lot better.

Over the years I came up with my own personal idea of what a sound endurance diet should might consist of. It took a lot of experimenting and was "hit or miss" for many years and I will be glad to share my thoughts on the subject with you. It's just one person's opinion, and you can certainly draw your own conclusions and take it or leave it. All I know is that with more attention to resting and a better diet I felt better and performed better when I was 45 than when I was 28.

Once I read in a book that was written many years ago by a Doctor Robert Hass that the proper balance of fats, proteins, and complex carbohydrates could actually make your blood younger. I think that's exactly what happened to me.

These are some of the diet ideas I shared with athletes who were taking on their first Ironman in my book "Ironstruck". In my mind they are just as valuable to the novice triathlete.

From all the reading I've done, and all the diets I've tried, I'm 100% certain that carbohydrates are the key to the ideal triathlon diet. I'm not talking simple carbohydrates like cookies, cake, and ice cream, but rather complex carbohydrates. If anything, I may have gone overboard on the carbohydrate consumption, but I seemed to be able to tolerate quite a high percentage of carbohydrates in my diet. It certainly isn't for everyone, but make sure that on a percentage basis your carbohydrates are always higher than your protein and fat intake.

Try and keep your protein and fat at about the same percentages. You might consider having a look at the diet by Doctor Sears. The doctor suggests a balance of 40% carbohydrates, 30% fat, and 30% protein or the 30-30-40 diet. My carbohydrate intake was much higher and I was closer to 75% carbohydrates, 10% fat, and 15% protein. This was much closer to the Doctor Hass diet formula I mentioned. His book was called "Eat to Win" if you are interested in learning more about it. I'm not even sure if it's still in print.

It is said that Dr. Hass devised Martina Navratilova's diet when she was beating the crap out of the world's best tennis players who were half her age. It was claimed that in her early 40's, she had the blood chemistry of an 18-year-old.

Some of the best carbohydrate sources are pasta, brown rice, whole wheat bread, pretty well all vegetables, and a controlled amount of fruit. Fruit does contain quite a lot of sugar, and you should try not to go overboard. At first I used to eat a lot of potatoes and white pasta until I found out that whole wheat pasta and sweet potatoes or yams were a healthier option.

For protein you have several preferable choices. Egg whites, low fat cottage cheese, plain yogurt, skim milk, white chicken and turkey meat, lean beef, and of course tuna and salmon are all good choices. Soy products and legumes have also become protein choices for many athletes who are vegetarian or want to restrict their meat intake.

129

The fat part of your diet will often be found in the protein you eat. There will be fat in the cottage cheese, chicken, turkey or beef you might eat. There will be fat in the 3 or 4 whole eggs you eat every week if you choose to. There will be a small amount of fat in the skim milk. Fish will also provide some fat, and I know it's expensive, but salmon is awesome for protein and fat (Omega oil).

The oil I preferred and have used for years is virgin olive oil. Try using a simple dressing of olive oil and red wine vinegar or lemon juice in your tossed salads. It's surprising how good salads can taste when the flavor of the vegetables is not masked by sugary dressings. Top your salad with cottage cheese and you have a great balance of complex carbohydrates, good fat, and protein.

Some notes: condiments (ketchup, mustard, mayonnaise, salad dressings etc) should be used sparingly. Cheddar cheese is fine, but try and stick to 6-8 ounces per week. Your best cheeses are hard cheeses and your first choice should be Parmesan (grated) for your pasta.

Peanut butter is okay in controlled amounts if you buy the real thing that has a half inch of oil on the top and is a pain to mix. At least you know you have made the right choice. It's the wrong choice if you have the peanut butter loaded with icing sugar just so it will be nice and smooth.

As far as your beverage choices, use skim milk as I mentioned above. Don't be afraid of aspartame in moderate quantities. It is a far better choice than sugar and allows you to use sweeteners like Equal in your coffee etc. It also means you can drink diet pop on occasion (with aspartame). Another really good choice is Crystal Lite as it is also sweetened with aspartame and not sugar should you prefer a sweeter option to plain water.

Beer or wine is okay in extreme moderation. Maybe three drinks a week and drink light beer. Getting rip-roaring drunk is not a great idea when you are training. It causes dehydration and could well ruin several days of training.

In many sports, and not just triathlon, athletes will train religiously for months or like I did, for years, and not realize their full potential because of an improper diet. I believe if you use my suggestions as a guideline, you will avoid having this happen to you.

You can always tweak a diet to be more compatible with foods you enjoy and have easy access to. The key is to always be aware of your balance of fats, proteins, and carbohydrates and see how your body reacts through the course of your training. Do you feel stronger, have more endurance, or recover better? Are you losing weight at the same time? These are all great indications that you are on the right track and have found a diet that works for you.

29. ATHLETICS AND NATUROPATHIC MEDICINE

by Guest Expert Derek Cook – BSc.H. N.D. (Naturopathic Doctor)

I met Derek at the Ironman Calgary 70.3 expo and had a long conversation with him and it was easy to see that he was passionate about his profession as a Naturopathic doctor and the opportunity it gave him to help others enjoy a longer, healthier, happier life. I'm so glad he agreed to share his thoughts on a well-rounded nutrition plan for the aspiring triathlete. -- Ray.

The old adage "you are what you eat" is incredibly important, not only in everyday life, but especially when you are training for a challenging event such as a triathlon. Naturopathic medicine strives to support the body by ensuring the conditions for optimum health. To achieve peak performance and reach your goals it is essential that you support your body. The type (protein, carbohydrates, and fats) and quality (whole vs processed, certified organic vs. non-organic) of foods you consume and adequate hydration are crucial for you to perform your best.

Whether you are an athlete or not, a goal should be to have a nutritious breakfast each and every morning, no exceptions. This is the case whether you train or not that day. Your body spends the entire night repairing and reconstructing the body and by morning it is starving for high quality nutrients. Breakfast is by far THE MOST IMPORTANT meal of the day. If you already eat breakfast, that's great! If not, it is time for you to start. You will feel and see the difference within weeks. Better concentration and increased energy will only be a few of the benefits.

Your body will be fueled up properly and ready to go.

What is a good breakfast? My personal favorite is the smoothie. It is tasty, quick and easy, and perfect to take on-the-go. It is packed with nutrition that your body desperately needs for all the upcoming exercise. I use my magic bullet (blender) to blend 1/3 of a cup of frozen berries (organic), 1/3 cup of organic yogurt, protein powder, and ½ to 1 whole banana (organic). I top it up for an 8-12 oz smoothie with equal parts of 100% fruit juice and rice milk. The protein powder should have all 20 amino acids, especially the 8 essential ones for adults (the ones your body can't make by itself): phenylalanine, valine, threonine, tryptophan, isoleucine, methionine, leucine and lysine. Methionine is incredibly important for regenerating the natural anti-oxidant system in the body to handle the harmful oxidants produced during exercise. Bottom line, breakfast should be packed with nutrients including protein and this smoothie is a perfect example.

If you are a vegetarian, it is extremely difficult to acquire all the essential amino acids in the proper amounts, in particular methionine and cysteine. You should also consider supplementing with B vitamins, especially B12. One way of getting your essential amino acids is by eating a whey protein supplement or egg whites.

Endurance athletes need double the protein requirement (1.3g/kg/day). For example, a 70 kg (154 lbs) man requires 91g protein/day and a 55 Kg (121 lbs) woman, 72g protein/day. This is because you can expect that about 5% of your energy during the event/training will be taken from your muscles - your body's protein stores. If you are a vegetarian and get most of your protein from non-meat, you will need 1.6g/kg/day (112g and 81g for above example) to ensure you get enough of the essential amino acids. If you are vegan, it is strongly recommended to use a protein supplement according to the vegetarian amounts.

Table 1: Foods and their amounts of protein when weighed raw.

Food	Weight	Amount of protein
*Lentils	175 g (raw)	50 g
*Kidney Beans	175 g (raw)	35 g
*Chickpeas	175 g (raw)	35 g
*Tofu	175 g (raw)	14 g
Chicken	175 g (raw)	40 g
Beef	150 g (raw)	25 g
Salmon	175 g (raw)	35 g
Egg	1 egg	6 g

*Note: plant sources of protein are low in methionine (essential amino acid) and cysteine.

Protein deficiency may show up as wasted appearance, bloating or swelling, increased cortisol /growth hormone, decreased insulin/thyroid hormone and frequent infections. On the other hand, overloading on too much protein may result in kidney problems, so more is not necessarily better. This is often seen with body builders.

Healthy fats are essential in dealing with the lactic acid build up that will eventually result from training and competing. When lactic acid builds up, it can lead to the production of arachidonic acid, causing inflammation (pain and cramping). Also, fats are an important part in cellular health, transportation and communication, all of which are critical, especially during an event.

Some healthy fats can be found in avocados, nuts (flax, pumpkin, sunflower and sesame), olive oil, borage oil and fish oils. It is recommended you eat a wide variety of the foods containing healthy oils to ensure you obtain them in sufficient quantities. It is always best to balance the source of your fat intake. Avoid burgers and fries, as they typically provide the unhealthy fats, saturated and trans fats, and promote inflammation. Trans fats form from unsaturated oils that are cooked at high heat. Never ever cook with oil! Instead, use water during cooking, then lower the heat and mix in the oil at the end. This will still give you the flavour, but the oil will stay in its natural, healthier form.

Whether to eat organic or non-organic foods is a huge debate. Everyone always asks, "Is it worth it"? This is highly subjective for each individual. Personally, I think it is worth it. The average person is exposed to over 50,000 chemicals a day and has at least 40-50 foreign chemicals in their body at any given time. These chemicals clog up normal cellular function, which usually translates into fatigue. So if you want a healthier body, support it by eating cleaner organic foods and support businesses that reduce chemical use.

As an added bonus to organic, it usually tastes better and has a higher nutrient content! Try it yourself, buy an organic orange and non-organic and taste the difference. In Canada, when the labels indicates "certified organic", it can be relied upon as the regulations are relatively strict now. Unfortunately, in the USA, certified organic labeling is not as reliable due to laxer regulations.

Are you getting enough water? Typically, a person (non-triathlete) needs about half their weight (in lbs) in ounces where 34 Oz (or 68 lbs) equals 1 liter. For example, if you weigh 136 lbs and were a non-athlete, you would need 2 liters of pure water (without adding anything to it) just to flush your body out properly. During exercise and competition events, your water intake will need to increase accordingly, depending on conditions. The rule of thumb is that your urine should be clear. This is also a time (just before, during and after training/event) where adding an electrolyte supplement to your water would be a good idea, since when you sweat, you lose a lot more than just water.

Endurance athletes use a tremendous amount of energy during training and events, and as a result they produce a lot of wastes (lactic acid, oxidants). Following a diet everyday that is rich in fruits and vegetables will ensure a high antioxidant status in the body. This will help to optimize cellular function and prevent damage, allowing for peak performance. Anti-oxidant supplements such as vitamins A, B, C, E, selenium, N-acetyl cysteine, glutathione and bioflavanoids - to name a few- are known to lower recovery time, but supplements are by no means a substitute for eating healthy. Typically, 50% of your food intake should be obtained from fruits and vegetables. It would also be wise to consult a Naturopathic Doctor regarding a specific anti-oxidant treatment for recovery.

These are some of the basic fundamentals to good health that are easy to transition into and they will make that difference for your performance. It is very important to feed and water your body properly. Your body will love you for it and you will be able to reach new heights!

"The doctor of the future will give no medicine but will interest his patients in the care of the human frame, in diet and in the cause and prevention of disease." – Thomas Edison

www.healthflow.ca

30. VITAMIN SUPPLEMENTS

For the most part, this is an area best left to experts, but I can share with you some of the vitamin supplements that I found enhanced my triathlon training and racing. There are many, many choices in today's marketplace as far as supplementing your diet, but the only ones I will mention are ones I have actually tried myself.

I always felt it was important to include the anti-oxidants vitamin C, vitamin E and selenium to my list of vitamins. Actually I would buy the vitamin C with selenium added. The main function of antioxidants appears to be to act as a deterrent to the forming of free radicals in your body when unsaturated fats are consumed.

For many triathletes, cold water swims are an issue, and it was something I struggled with over the years until I came across the vitamin supplement pantothenic acid. Apparently it plays an important role in energy production. I also discovered that pantothenic acid is a key antioxidant for athletes who compete in extreme conditions that include cold water. If you do purchase it, what you ask for is calcium pentathonate, the calcium salt of pantothenic acid. I really felt that it made a big difference to me in warding of the effects of swimming in cold water races.

If you research pantothenic acid, you will find that endurance swimmers have had success using this supplement while swimming the English Channel and I doubt that water conditions can get much worse for endurance swimmers than they are in that part of the world.

I also noticed an improvement in energy levels when I used branch chain amino acids. Amino acids also function as anti-oxidants and help compensate if your diet is a bit lacking in protein. I was on such a high carbohydrate diet, that branch chain amino acids seemed like an ideal choice for me.

My all-time favorite for a supplement over the years was L'carnatine. I could take this one and three weeks later be five pounds lighter. I also notice a marked improvement in my energy levels and recovery from training. It's *very* expensive, but well worth it. If you can find it, I would use it. I believe its available over the counter in the U.S., but now has become "by prescription only" in Canada. That's a pretty good indication that it works. Here again, I would advise that you do your own due diligence.

So there you have it. That's the vitamin package I preferred using in the run-up to my races. I don't believe it's necessary to use most of these vitamins on a year-round basis, but it's a good idea in the final months leading up to your big race. I also believe that supplements are more effective if you pick your spots. It took years of hit and miss to finally come up with this combination. All the doses except for vitamin C and selenium were 500 mg. I would take more (1000) vitamin C with 50 mg of selenium added.

Anyone doing the demanding training required to become a triathlete should seriously consider vitamin supplements.

NOTE: Don't fall into this trap ... If something works really well for you, don't assume that more will be even better. Stay with the amount that seemed to make a difference.

31. FOOD FOR THOUGHT

Over the years I have come across some nutrition ideas that seemed a bit different, but really seem to work. I thought I would share these two with you and you can give these suggestions a try ... or not, whatever flicks your switch. Personally, I like to experiment because you just never know how your body might react and how it might really make a positive difference until you try.

COCONUT OIL: I had a lot of success with coconut oil and its something I would certainly look into. I used about 4-5 tablespoons a day in my cooking and smoothies and noticed several things. First of all, I lost an extra five pounds that I didn't even realize I had to lose as I was pretty lean. I also noticed a noticeable increase in energy and an improvement in my endurance. Aside from mother's milk, coconut oil is pretty well the only source of lauric acid in the world. For some reason it speeds up the body's metabolism and promotes weight loss when used in combination with regular physical activity. In other words, it seems to be perfect for a triathlete in training. It wouldn't hurt to give it a try for a few months and see if it does anything for you.

COFFEE: Apparently there is good reason for coffee drinker to perk up as it seems their daily dose of Joe might not be such a bad thing after all. There have been rumblings for several years now about the possible benefits of coffee. Today it's been all over the news that up to six cups of coffee a day not only won't hurt you, but is actually good for you.

This revelation after a 20 year study of male and female coffee drinkers.

That might explain why many athletes have long believed that coffee drinkers will actually perk up physically and perform better.

Most of us link coffee with caffeine and the buzz and lift it gives us as we make our way through our busy lives and indeed it does seem that coffee drinkers perk up on a more regular basis than those who abstain. However, it has been found that coffee might also contain beneficial antioxidants that help fight off the free radicals that invade our bodies on a daily basis. In the study it was found there was a lower incidence of heart disease in those involved in the study when compared with national averages.

Even this coffee lover would be hard-pressed to put back 6 cups of coffee a day even if it is true that coffee drinkers are perked up by this practice. My personal take on it is to enjoy a cup or two (or maybe 3) of your favorite coffee per day, and not go overboard. I'm sure like with most things in life that offer any semblance of enjoyment, moderation is the key.

It does bring up an interesting point, however. Like the pro triathlete who insisted on his 2 or 3 cups of strong, black coffee every morning before his Ironman race. I remember two years in a row when he finished 6th overall in Ironman Canada. Makes you think there is something in it.

Also, caffeine is a banned substance when it comes to Olympic athletes, so that in itself might tell you that there is some validity to the fact that it might harbor some advantage for triathletes. Of course I don't think a few cups of coffee is enough to get anyone into "hot water" but caffeine pills might.

I have tried coffee myself before 10 KM races in the past and did find that I got a bit of a boost from it in the early going of the race, and others report that it was a big help to their endurance and drinking coffee did indeed perk them up physically as well as mentally.

I just thought I would pass this on, because like the egg, it seems like all the bad press for coffee is coming to an end. I would say enjoy your coffee, but use good judgment and don't overdo it, as most likely even the coffee drinker who enjoys a single cup of coffee a day will feel a bit perked up. As far as incorporating jolts of strong coffee into your race morning preparations, I would strongly recommend testing it out in training first. Some people have adverse effects from coffee and although it may perk some coffee drinkers up, there are others it may not agree with and it might make them grind to a halt.

32. RACE-DAY FOOD & DRINK

I have come to believe that this is perhaps the most analyzed, discussed, misunderstood, and confusing topic in the world of triathlon.

If you talk to ten different people, you will probably get ten different opinions. I suppose that makes sense, because what works great for one person when it comes to eating and hydration just before and during a race might not work for the other nine.

I will gladly share my thoughts on the subject, but whatever you do always remember this: If at all possible, don't eat or drink anything on race day that you have not tried out in training.

DRINKING: It makes sense that the longer the race, the more important the drinking and eating becomes. For instance I never, ever took a drink or food during a 10k road race, but drank plenty during a marathon. It's important to be properly hydrated before a race of any distance, and for 10k races I made sure I properly hydrated on the day before the race. For me the race was usually over in 38 minutes or so and slowing down to take a cup of water was a distraction and would normally upset my stomach at those speeds and was not a help to me. It would certainly be a different story if someone planned on being out on a 10km run course for more than an hour. In that case, it would be important to keep well-hydrated.

Even the shortest of triathlons requires you to be sufficiently hydrated before and during the race, because you will always be doing three events. That means that keeping your body properly fueled and hydrated will play a major role in how you feel and perform in all three disciplines. It will also have an impact on how well you recover in the days following the race. It's crucial to drink enough in the days leading up to the race. If your race is Sunday, begin drinking extra on the Wednesday or Thursday at the latest. Once your urine is clear and copious you are pretty well where you want to be.

It is not true that more water is better. As a matter of fact there is more and more discussion these days about the dangers of drinking too much and flushing essential minerals out of your body.

Your goal should be to reach a proper level of hydration as I just described and then maintain that until race day. I strongly suggest you avoid drinking a lot on race morning. There is nothing worse than water sloshing around in your stomach during the swim. If you have hydrated properly in the preceding days you will not need a lot of water on race morning.

The object during the race is to replace fluid in your body as you use it. If you wait until you get thirsty, it's most likely too late and it's hard to catch up. It's best to drink in small amounts *often* rather than large amounts a few times. This is where your triathlon watch will come in handy. You can have your timer all set up to beep every 15 or 20 minutes during the bike and it will remind you to take a drink at regular intervals..

It's best not to drink the moment you get out of the water. Give your body time to adjust from being horizontal to vertical. I would wait for 10 or 15 minutes into the bike leg, take your first drink, and then start your timer.

If you keep up with your hydration during the bike, it will be easy to keep it up during the run. Just take a drink at every aid station.

You might choose to use a replacement drink as well. The longer the race, the more important this becomes as replacement drinks are meant to replenish the sodium and potassium levels in your body. There are many different replacement drinks on the market today and it's best to try different ones in your training to see how they work for you. This is especially important on those hot training days that might emulate your race day. The hotter the temperature, the more crucial a well-thought-out drinking strategy becomes.

Personally, I had the most success with a product called Cytomax. It was a hard-core cyclist who suggested it to me many years ago when it was only available in the U.S. so I would get it by mail-order. (It was so long ago, there was no Internet to speak of, so I did it by phone). You will find that Cytomax is now available in Canada, but like many products that work well, the ingredients are changed so much to meet Canadian standards that the product loses its effectiveness. I would suggest ordering it from the U.S. if you live in Canada.

Anyway, it was the year that I used Cytomax that I had my best result on the bike. During your race you can alternate between water and your replacement drink or take a little of each when you drink.

EATING: Just like drinking, it's wise to begin loading up on carbohydrates several days before your race. Personally, I always made it a point to eat my last big meal on the eve of the race late in the afternoon as opposed to the evening. I tried to be done eating by 4 P.M. This ensured that my food was properly digested before the swim start the next morning. My breakfast of choice on most race mornings was whole wheat toast with honey (easy on the honey), one banana, and tea. I would have that 3 hours before the race start, so it meant getting up early.

Your glycogen stores will be nicely topped up from the days before the race if you carbo-loaded properly.

In short sprint triathlons and the Olympic distance, you will not need huge amounts of food. If you get off the bike in good shape you most likely will not need any food during the run. You should have eaten enough on the bike course so that it's not necessary or really wise to be eating too much on the run course. By then it's too late to do you much good anyway, and most likely will upset your stomach. A few power gels might be okay to get you through the late stages of the run.

Even in the Ironman distance there has been a misconception about how much to eat on the bike course. To my way of thinking, it's not a great idea to be eating in the late stages of and Ironman bike course. It's really all about consuming sufficient calories and if you eat something in the hour or so before getting off the bike, your body will not digest it soon enough to do you any good. Chances are it will cause you to bonk and have an energy crash.

I believe the secret is to eat early on in the bike. Eat food that will take a while to be assimilated. For instance an energy bar or gel is not a great choice in the early stages of the bike. A power gel is absorbed into your blood stream too quickly and is usually best for short bursts of energy.

I had my best results eating whole wheat bagels with peanut butter and honey. Two of them cut in half was just right for even the 112 mile Ironman distance. I mean, take a look at what this provides. It's just what I talked about earlier. A good source of complex carbohydrates in the whole wheat bagel, protein in the bagel and the peanut butter, and fat in the peanut butter, and the honey to make it all taste really great and a little extra boost of energy.

I ate those bagels, drank Cytomax and water, and just took a cup of water at every aid station (every mile) in the marathon (no food) and ran a 3:34

marathon in an Ironman and had the best recovery from a race I had ever had.

I'm thinking that just one of those bagels might be perfect for you for a sprint tri or Olympic distance. Just be sure to eat early on in the bike and not in the later stages, as any food you eat just before you begin your run will most likely do more harm than good.

Anyway, those are my thoughts on the subject and what worked for me. As I said, the key is to experiment long before the race and see what works best for you.

33. OUT OF TOWN RACES

One thing I really enjoy about the sport of triathlon is that you get to travel pretty well anywhere these days and take part in a race. It is truly a sport for the world. I have so many memories of people I have met from places like New Zealand, Australia, Mexico, the U.S., the U.K., Japan, and many other countries.

The best part is that you are all on the same journey and basically speak the same language in a sense.

I remember one Ironman Canada race in particular when I was beating back the demons and willing myself around Skaha Lake in the late stages of the marathon. I came up on a Japanese athlete. I didn't think it was possible, but I think he was in worse shape than I was. He looked over at me and said something in Japanese and I didn't need a translator to tell me that "I think I'm going to die" was pretty much in the ball park of what he said. As I slowly pulled away from him I heard him shout out something else that was no doubt along the lines of "good luck, have a great race!" Well, or perhaps "you crazy white guy! Thanks for sticking with me!"

Anyway, it's always such a treat to interact with others who are sharing your journey regardless of how long your triathlon is or where it's taking place.

However, for your first few triathlons I believe it's in your best interest to race close to home rather than at an out-of-town destination. If you are new to the sport, there are many good reasons to make the most of the "home-field" advantage.

Of course every city and town is different, but if you have an ideal distance triathlon that you can enter that's only a 15 or 20 minute drive from home, these are just a few of the reasons why it's a great way to kick off your triathlon career.

TRAIN ON THE ROUTE: What better place to train than to go out on the course weeks and even months before the race and do some training on it? If the swim happens to be in a lake, then you can even do a few of your very first open-water swims out on the swim course (with a friend).

EAT AT HOME: Whenever you travel, you have to pay attention to what you are eating if you have no choice but to eat in the local restaurants. When you think about, you might be training for months and most likely develop certain foods and eating habits that work perfectly for you. Then here you are in the most important days leading up to your race, eating food you are not used to and did not prepare yourself. I had food poisoning once two days before an Ironman and it forced me out of the race right near the end of the swim. If you *must* travel out of town, always try and get a fully-equipped kitchenette and buy and prepare your own food.

SLEEP AT HOME: It's quite normal to toss and turn in the last few nights leading up to a big race, but at least if you are at home you will be used to the bed and will be as comfortable as possible.

EASY ACCESS: You won't need hours to get to the race venue and spend time trying to familiarize yourself as to where the heck everything is. You will know the best places to park, where the transition areas are, and where the race starts and ends without having to search around.

AFTER THE RACE: Chances are you will be really proud and happy after you cross the finish line, but at the same time a bit sore and tired.

You will find it quite a relief to be only a short ride from the comfort of your own home.

I remember once when I was in the late stages of training for an Ironman that I had planned to do my own makeshift shorter triathlon as part of my training. I entered a local 10k race that was coming up in town. The race start was only an easy 10 minute jog from my home. So I got up early, did an hour of biking on my wind-trainer, jogged down to the race start, ran the race, went to the pool by my place and swam 2000 meters and then went to the awards ceremony. It was making use of the home field advantage that comes with racing in your own city.

SUPPORT: If you are just starting out in this amazing sport and it's your first race, by racing in your home town you will most likely have more friends and family who will be able to come out to the race and share your big day. Never underestimate the power of your support team to propel you to your ultimate goal.

There are more and more triathlons springing up all over the world all the time. It's so cool to have the opportunity to plan a triathlon career that can take you from the interior of British Columbia, to Hawaii, Malaysia, or New Zealand. You can almost bet that every city that sponsors an Ironman event will have lots of shorter races in and around the area. This would give you an opportunity to take some vacation time and do your own shorter race and then check out an Ironman event. Sometimes that's all it takes to inspire people to start training for their first Ironman.

For instance, on one weekend you could take part in the Kelowna Apple Triathlon in B.C. and the next weekend you could be a spectator or volunteer at Ironman Canada in Penticton. In between you could spend some vacation time in an incredibly beautiful part of the world.

I believe you would be hard-pressed to even find a city in North America that does not have at least one or most likely several triathlons in and around their area.

There is so much to look forward in this sport as your career progresses, but it's to your advantage to ease yourself into triathlon and learn all you can about it on your home turf before hitting the highway.

34. RACE DAY LOOMS

Time marches on. Sometimes it marches so fast that panic begins to set in. Ten months ago you might have been at peace with taking on your first triathlon, but as the weeks fly by and your race is looming on the horizon, the first inklings of self-doubt are beginning to creep into your thoughts.

Am I ready? Am I in good enough shape? Can I do this? Will I even finish? Will I make a fool of myself in front of the whole world? Is this a mistake? Should I change my name and disappear?

Well, you get the picture.

Believe me, this is all perfectly normally and something that pretty well every novice triathlete most likely goes though in one form or another.

Of course you will have doubts, but you can dispel those doubts by the realization of how far you have come to reach this point.

Think back to when becoming a triathlete seemed like an impossible dream. Maybe you had to learn how to swim, quit smoking, or lose weight. You have come so far, and yet doubt your sanity about answering the starting gun of your triathlon.

That's like winning the lottery and chastising yourself for buying the ticket.

You began to win when you picked up a books like this or were moved by something you witnessed or heard that inspired to make a change ...

155

and you did. You have yourself to thank for that. Inspiration provides a nudge for that first baby step, but the long strides down the road of success, self-esteem, and accomplishment come from the spirit, determination, and strength you have within.

Maybe you just had to discover that it was there.

You have come so far!

Sure, there's the possibility that your race might not go as smoothly as you hoped it would. That's all part of the learning experience. That doesn't change the fact that you have come a long, long way. Besides, if you look at the worst that could possibly happen it puts everything in prospective. You might think that not finishing the race is the worse thing that could happen to you.

On the other hand, I really believe the worst thing that could happen is that you really want to give triathlon a try, but don't go down this road in the first place because you doubt that you have what it takes. You simply cannot lose when you are learning new skills, gaining a higher level of fitness, building self-esteem, and improving your overall health.

Crossing the finish line is the icing on the cake, but it's just part of the cake.

You don't become a triathlete when you cross the finish line for the first time. You become a triathlete the very moment you lace up your running shoes, hop on a bike, and sign up for your first swimming lesson.

The secret to having success on your race day is to always keep in mind that you can never truly fail, because you are already a winner even before the starting gun sounds.

I recall the story of the triathlete from South Africa who had failed to finish the Ironman in Mandella Bay on his first five attempts. He told me in an email that he just loved being part of the experience and how it inspired him to keep improving and keep believing in himself. Every race was a revelation for him and an inspiration to try harder to reach his goal of the Ironman finish line.

It was a thrill to hear from him months later when he declared that he was now an "Ironman." To me, his success story began in his very first attempt when he showed the courage and determination to take on the Ironman challenge. He grew in so many ways by taking on the challenge over and over again and not ever seeing himself as a failure, but rather as someone on a journey to a better way of life. A journey that in reality, had no end.

As you await your race, take pride in all you have accomplished to get there. Embrace the euphoria of sharing your experience with others who have traveled the same road. As you look ahead to your coming race, just remember that on that day you will be part of something special and rather than dread it, welcome it with open arms as you continue your journey toward becoming a spectacular new you.

35. ONE MORE SLEEP

All right! It's race day tomorrow!

So what should you be paying attention to as you prepare for tomorrow morning's race start?

Well, hopefully you have taken care of things like registration and you have your race package. You will most likely find a sheet in there with important information about race-day. It might involve parking, the awards ceremony, your exact starting time (some races have swim wave starts) and any other pertinent information you might find helpful.

You should also find your race numbers in your race bag and information on where to pin them. In most triathlons your race number goes on your back for the bike leg and your front for the run. You don't have to worry about the swim because you will also find a swim cap in the bag with your race number on it.

Most races these days use timing chips and that will be provided as well. The idea is to put it on race morning. It goes around your ankle and times your entire race as you go in and out of transition and cross the timing mats.

THINK AHEAD: The eve of the race is the time to prepare all your gear, water, and food for the next day. The goal is to make race morning as relaxing as possible. If you are looking all over for your goggles, your swim cap, or timing chip 30 minutes before the swim start, all you will be doing is stressing yourself and burning off valuable energy.

EATING AND DRINKING: I can't stress enough how crucial it is avoid foods that are usually spicy, foods that you are unaccustomed to, or over-eating in general. This is not the time to be stressing your digestive system. Stick with food that is easily digested, fairly bland, and not loaded with fiber. Have your eating over by early evening at the latest and this will give your digestive system lots of time to do its work.

It's the same thought process with drinking. It you have come across a new drink at the expo that promises to propel you to the finish line faster than a speeding bullet, save it for the next race when you have had a chance to try it out in training. Introducing new food and drink into your diet just before – or on race day – is a recipe for disaster.

It's also important to avoid over-drinking on the eve of the race. As I mentioned earlier, more is not necessarily better when it comes to hydration. If you have hydrated and carbo-loaded properly in the days prior to your race, you can feel confident that you are ready to go.

Stay out of the sun as much as possible, as this will sap your energy and could mess up your hydration preparations. This is not the time to be wandering around an outdoor expo in the blazing heat. It's actually time better spent in the coolness and calmness of your lodging and reminding yourself how far you have come in your amazing journey.

Find a quiet place and use the visualization techniques I suggested and focus on the day ahead. Visualize your long, strong, smooth swim stroke, your perfect spinning circles on the bike, and crossing the finish line and realizing the goal you have worked so hard to accomplish.

36. ATTITUDE IS EVERYTHING

by guest expert Steve King

I'm sure I'm not the only triathlete who has fond memories of being called into the finish line by Steve King. In fact, thousands of triathletes around the world have been in the final stages of their race and strained to hear Steve's voice in the distance. Steve was their "beacon in the night" and their reassurance that the finish line was not far away. Steve has a way of buoying the spirit and injecting energy where once there was none. I'm sure I speak for many, many people when I say.."Thanks, Steve, for what you bring to every event you are involved in and for being such a big part of the fond memories that will stay with us for a lifetime." – Ray.

There is one thing that we can determine no matter what challenges we may choose to undertake or are confronted with, and that is the attitude that we can carry with us.

If we choose an "Attitude of Gratitude", then it will often allow these experiences to just FLOW and be FUN.

In terms of goal-setting, it is often said that our goals need to be S.M.A.R.T. – that is, Specific, Measurable, Agreeable, Realistic and Time-sensitive. The sport of triathlon fits perfectly with those criteria.

Here we are at a time when many have not known a world without the sport of triathlon – whether from the grass roots events that sprang up in the early 1980's to its inclusion in the 2000 Olympic Games. Canada is fortunate to be able to boast the inaugural gold medalist and 2008 silver medalist in the form of Simon Whitfield. However, it was not even a foreseeable goal for him when he started his career via the Kids of Steel program. Goals and possibilities have opened up dramatically for the newcomers to the sport.

When young, we initially got involved in activities purely for fun and friendship. As adults, especially in the sport of triathlon, involvement is now more often connected to a particular challenge (Try a Tri, My First Tri, Relay, Sprint, Olympic, 70.3 or Ironman distances) or on behalf of a particular charity (Team in Training, Cops for Cancer, Team Diabetes etc.) For many, the initial involvement in the sport was for gaining some level of competence and not for competition or comparing performance to others.

Performance can be broken down into:

- Ability – the potentialities that are developed and refined by knowledge and experience.

- Focus – taking notice of just one thing by narrowing your attention to other input, including the modulation of energy levels.

- Motivation – the reason we do something. It incorporates perspective, the ability to generate short and long term goals, and the flexibility to move from one to another.

- Attitude or Mindset as well as Energy State.

Often the biggest fear is the fear of failure, but winning is truly independent of the outcome, and as someone once said, "sometimes you win more by losing!"

The one thing we know for sure is that none of us will get out of this alive, so we might as well make our life something that we truly want!

Some good personal goal-setting questions include:

- What dreams did you have as a child that you have given up on?
- Who do you wish you could be like?
- What would you like to do that you haven't been able to do yet?
- What would you do/attempt/be if your success was guaranteed?
- What would you do if you were brave?

We are fearful of making a mistake or beginning something new, but there is always a result – it is what you do with the result that counts. What are the lessons from the experience that you can take away with you?

Bear in mind that activity absorbs anxiety, and "All stress is internally generated by one's attitudes." (Dr. David Hawkins)

Exercise is the chain that links us to the chariot of well-being. Well-being means happiness, but happiness is also an attitude, and the best attitude is one of gratitude. May you choose to TRI to keep FIT.

Stephen King, 575 Burns St., Penticton, B.C., V2A 4W9,

Tel: (250) 490-9159 Fax: (250) 492-4058

E-mail stking@vip.net Website www2.vip.net/~stking/

Steve King holds a B.Sc. degree in Health and Human Services, and is a Registered Clinical Counselor. He is an avid runner, race-walker and triathlete who has held six national age group records, has raced at Ironman and Ultraman triathlon distances and has been a member of Canada's national 100km team. In 2001 he became only the second Canadian ever to complete the grueling Badwater Death Valley 135 mile run. He was the publisher of "Tri-Fit Quarterly", a national triathlon magazine, author of a triathlon training log and CBC`s colour commentator for the sport of triathlon. He is also the race announcer for many sports events including Ironman Canada, with an avid interest in healthy balance and wholism. Steve has worked at Pathways Addictions Resource Center in Penticton since 1989 and he authored a book on energy psychology entitled, *"Rapid Recovery",* co-edited *"Running in the Zone",* and is a contributing writer to *Gin & Platonic and Other Short Stories with a Twist.*

37. COMMON RACE MORNING MISTAKES

There's a lot to remember on race morning, and the anxiety and excitement of the moment can easily cause you to make mistakes. Many of the same mistakes are made over and over again by novice triathletes. I'm really familiar with them, because I made most of them myself in the course of my triathlon career.

Here are a few suggestions that will make your race go a lot smoother.

RISE AND SHINE: The last thing you want to do on race morning is get a late start and have to rush through your pre-race preparations. It makes more sense to me to ensure that you get a really good night's sleep 2 days before your race. In other words if your race is on Sunday, Friday night is the night you want to sleep soundly and if possible, even sleep in.

There's a good chance you will toss and turn the eve of the race anyway, so you might just as well plan on being up early on race morning. By doing this you can take your time preparing and there is less chance of making mistakes and forgetting something important.

EATING AND DRINKING: This topic always comes up and that's because how you handle your eating and drinking during training, race week, race-eve, race morning, and during the race itself will impact your overall performance and go a long way toward determining how your race day unfolds. Always remember that what you eat and drink is your body's fuel. It's hard to train like a Ferrari if you fuel yourself like a '55 Ford.

Hopefully you finished your eating fairly early the night before the race as suggested and are not still digesting the beer and pizza you had at midnight.

For your race morning breakfast, you might try my pre-race favorite of two slices of brown toast with honey, one banana and a cup of tea. Or perhaps you have a light breakfast in mind that works for you, but keep it simple and keep it light. Regardless, have it early and don't make the mistake of eating too close to the swim start.

The same goes for drinking. If you have hydrated properly in the days leading up to the race, you will not need to be drinking a lot on race morning. It would make more sense to sip on a water bottle over the course of the morning if you feel the need, and stop drinking in the hour leading up to the race.

I suppose everyone is different, but I discovered early in my career how uncomfortable it can be to have an undigested breakfast and copious amounts of water in your system during the swim. It may not be a factor in the relative calm of a pool swim, but the open water is an entirely different story.

PRE-SET YOUR BIKE GEAR: I was a spectator at a recent triathlon and saw first hand what can happen when a bike is set in the wrong gear before the race start. This particular race had cyclists heading straight uphill as they left the transition area after the swim. It seemed like every other rider had their bike set in a big gear and struggled to get up the hill.

Regardless of whether there is a hill at the start or not, leave your bike in the easiest gear before the race starts. This will give you more control as you mount the bike and get your feet locked into the pedals. Once you are settled, you can easily shift into a bigger gear.

WETSUIT SWEATS: Wetsuits are designed to fit snug and keep you warmer in the water. As soon as you zip them up prior to the swim start, you will feel your body begin to heat up. Avoid making the mistake of zipping them up too soon. It the race start is 30 or 40 minutes away, you will become overheated and uncomfortable if you zip your suit right up.

It would make more sense to put your wetsuit on and pull it up as far as your waist until the race start is around 10 minutes or so away. That gives you lots of time to slip your arms in, pull your suit up over your shoulders and have someone zip you up.

THE INS AND OUTS: When you first stand up as you exit the water after completing the swim, chances are good that you will be a little dizzy. This is natural as your body adjusts from being horizontal to vertical.

To make things easier for yourself, make a note of where your bike is from the point where you enter transition from the swim. Be at the race start early so you can check things out and get your bearings.

Don't forget you will be walking your bike until you reach the designated mounting zone before heading out onto the bike course. Most likely it will be busy and a bit crowded with other cyclists. It makes it much easier if you know exactly where you are supposed to be going.

Just take your time and relax and be aware of others around you who might be a bit unsteady on their bikes in the loading area and you'll be fine.

38. CHILLING OUT

I just have to tell this story because it has an important lesson in it that might prove useful to you. It goes a long way toward explaining how "chilling out" and relaxing the night before, and the morning of the big race can have a profound effect on how your day unfolds.

As usual, I had trained for months for the upcoming marathon. I was all ready to go and felt I had done everything right. I had eased off on the training in the preceding few weeks and was coasting into the Sunday morning marathon that was going to take place in my city the next day.

For some reason, I started to feel very odd on the day before the race and my strength seemed to disappear. I was really listless and had no idea what was going on, but I knew there was no way I was going to be able to run a marathon in the morning the way I felt.

I went to bed about 11 P.M. with the thought in my head that I would just sleep in as I didn't have to get up early for the 7 A.M. marathon start.

As it happened, I woke up about 5 A.M. anyway. I got out of bed and thought, "I don't feel as bad this morning as I did last night." So I decided to go out for an easy jog on the bike path beside the river. It didn't feel too bad at all and I decided that since I had payed the entry and the race start was only about an 8 minute drive away, I would slide on over and perhaps run a few kilometers of the race and see how things went. I reasoned that if I felt okay I could just run easily and use the race as a long training run and not worry about my finish time.

I put on my running gear, pinned my number on, and drove over to the race. I managed to find a parking spot about 3 blocks away and walked over to the starting area. Everybody was already behind the starting line and with the race gun less than 2 minutes away I wandered over on and found a spot back in the pack. My heart-rate was probably around 75 bpm as I was completely relaxed. At the same time I was aware of the pre-race tension in the air that emanated from the six hundred or so runners who were on pins and needles anticipating the race start.

The gun went off, and as usual there was an adrenaline-fueled dash down the street. Except for me, I guess because I was in no hurry to get anywhere. I already had it fixed in my mind that I would be taking it easy so there was none of the usual race-morning stress and anticipation.

Then a funny thing happened.

I passed by the first mile marker and it was a leisurely 7:30 pace. I didn't feel too bad and I kept the same comfortable pace because after all, I was just supposed to be taking it easy. Then I was at the 10km mark and then the halfway mark and really began to feel strong.

It was about then that I thought I might as well make a race of it and started to pick up the pace a little. I began to pass people by the dozens. They were all slowing down and I was speeding up.

Before I knew it I was at the 37k mark and more and more people were walking and shuffling along as they began to run out of gas. I looked at my watch and thought "Wow! That's not a bad time! It was then that it struck me that I had a chance of hitting the 3:15 time that I had originally set as my goal weeks before.

Now I picked it up again and was amazed at how good I felt. I ran at that speed all the way to the finish line and finished in a time of just over 3:12.

When I look back on that marathon now, it's pretty clear to me what happened that day.

First of all, I was looking through Ironman champion Mark Allen's triathlon training book one day and read how his wife (Julie Moss) was training for a big marathon and a few days before the race Mark asked her how she felt. She answered that she felt terrible and Mark responded: "Perfect! That's just where you want to be." Apparently it's quite common to feel crappy as you taper and virtually stop training for an upcoming race after training like a gladiator for months. It's a chemical response from your body as it adjusts from hard training to the virtual inactivity of the late stages of a taper.

I had never really experienced it before so wasn't prepared for it. In reality, I was doing everything right and was all set for a good race, but I just didn't know it.

By chilling out and taking all the stress off myself I unknowingly set myself up perfectly for the marathon.

Just think about it.

The night before the race there was no stress because I thought there would be no race for me. The morning of the race I was relaxed and on a whim decided to take in the race and just go easy and have fun, and it served to keep my heart rate at rock bottom levels and was the *perfect* way to answer the starting gun. Going out easy gave my body time to ease into the race, and it responded perfectly when I began to ask more of it in the late stages.

In reality, that's the way a person should go into every single race, no matter what level they are racing at. It stands to reason that you are saving tons of energy by being relaxed before your race. It sets the tone for the entire event and will make it a much more enjoyable and successful experience.

It was an important lesson for me and was the blueprint for how I approached big races in the years to follow. It's something important to keep in mind as you prepare for your triathlon.

39. PACE IS THE KEY

From the very beginning of my venture into the world of athleticism from the depths of couch potatoism, (you learned a new word today) I have had suggestions, training tips, and racing secrets whispered into my ear from other athletes, interested bystanders, books, and just about any other source you can think of.

I have learned over the years that those four words "pace is the key" that were shared with me back in 1977 as I joined a veteran marathoner in a long run along the river pathway in Calgary, was perhaps the most important advice anyone has ever given me over the years.

I just didn't realize it at the time.

Soon after that day, I found myself embroiled in a new and exciting journey as I transcended from the couch of lost dreams and hopelessness to the start line of my first marathon within a matter of 8 months.

I ran that day with joy and abandon as fast as I could from the second the starting gun sounded. It was a such a revelation to have made this momentous transition in my life, and the euphoria of the moment had me on an impossible to sustain 2:45 marathon pace at the halfway mark.

The wind flowed through my hair, my feet had wings – and at about mile eighteen, my face was firmly embedded in the "wall" that somehow magically appeared out of nowhere. I came to a screeching halt and learned up close and personal just how painful a poorly paced race can be. However, I was determined that day and eventually crossed the line of my first ever marathon in 3 hours and 28 minutes. As I look back on that day, I realize just how amazing that time was under the circumstances, and just how shockingly fast it might have been had I run smarter.

It took me many, many more years to fully grasp the importance of those words, "pace is the key."

Ultimately, it really doesn't matter if you are a world champion 10,000 meter runner, an Olympic marathoner, or a novice triathlete, how you pace yourself will ultimately be the biggest determining factor in how your event unfolds.

It is vitally important to pace yourself *according to your experience and athletic ability*. If you let yourself get caught up in the early race's adrenaline-charged atmosphere and leave the starting line of any race at a pace you cannot possibly sustain for the duration of the event, I can pretty well guarantee that you *will* pay for it at some point later in the race.

It has happened to people in every 10k, marathon, or Ironman race I have ever been involved in. It happened to me countless times until I finally clued in. It goes a long ways toward explaining why my marathon and 10k times became faster as I grew older and smarter.

For example, I loved 10k road races and at one time adopted a strategy of making the first mile of every 10k race my slowest. I accelerated at the 1 mile mark, the halfway mark, and at the 1 mile to go mark and made my last mile my fastest. So when I ran a first mile of around 6 minutes, hundreds of people would take off in front of me.

At the mile mark, the majority of them were already beginning to slow down as I accelerated for the first time. From that point on, it was normal for me to not be passed by anyone all the way to the finish line. I was the one doing the passing as everyone else was slowing down when I was speeding up.

This can provide tons of self-confidence and motivation in the final run to the finish line, because in reality you can be just as strong, or stronger at the end of your race as you were when the gun went off. It's a huge psychological lift to be in that position.

It's not just about how fast you finish the race, or how many people you pass, but also about how much better you will feel and how much more you will enjoy the *experience* of your race if you pace yourself according to your ability and experience and don't get swept up in the euphoria of the moment when the starting gun sounds.

If just one thing sticks in your mind from this book as you begin your triathlon journey, make sure this it. It is one of the most valuable things you will ever learn as an athlete.

"PACE IS THE KEY."

40. THE OPEN WATER SWIM

There's a good chance you will be feeling very apprehensive about the swim start of your first few triathlons. I say that because there are so many people who venture into the sport being very poor swimmers or perhaps like myself, having to learn how to swim from square one.

It can be a daunting experience, and I know exactly where you're coming from. In all honesty, there is not a lot you can do in your initial swim lessons or training that will completely prepare you for a triathlon swim start. However, it's your lucky day, because the main reason I wrote this book is to help you to enjoy *all* aspects of your triathlon, and not just survive it.

Hopefully you have taken my advice and not taken on a lot of food and water in the hour or so before the swim start. If you have prepared properly in the days preceding the race, it's really unnecessary and might possibly make your swim uncomfortable.

As I suggested, the best time to zip your wetsuit up completely is about 10 minutes before the swim start. This will prevent you from overheating and becoming uncomfortable.

The tendency for most people is to stand on the shore or perhaps knee-deep in the water and then immerse themselves completely when the starting gun sounds, or very soon after. This can cause a problem if the water is on the cold side. Wearing a wet suit does not mean water does not seep inside of the suit. It does not protect your head and neck from

177

the initial chill. Some people will choose to wear a "thermal cap" under their race swim cap for extra warmth. This is not a bad idea at all, but like everything else pertaining to equipment or eating strategies, be sure to try a thermal cap out in your training. There will be a bit of a different sensation from a regular swim came as the thermal variety will cover your ears.

The shock of colder water can take your breath away. The experience will be very different than your pool training or the training you did in open water that was much warmer and much less crowded, but by taking a few easy steps you can make the whole experience much less traumatic.

In the last two minutes or so before the swim start, immerse yourself completely in the water and get that initial shock out of the way. Let your body slowly adjust to the temperature of the water and it won't feel nearly as bad and there will be no initial shock from the cold when the gun sounds.

 Almost without fail, novice triathletes go into the swim without a plan, and that's the biggest reason for their pre-swim apprehension. Go into the race with a workable swim plan.

Unless you are a super-fast swimmer, it's best to wait 10 seconds or so and pick an outside line away from the mass of swimmers. If the course is clockwise, keep all the other swimmers on your right. If it's counter-clockwise, keep them on your left. By being on the outside, you will be able to maintain a long, smooth stroke that is not being interrupted by swimmers running into you or swimming over top of you.

Every time you breathe you can look over at the other swimmers and you can key on them. By that I mean they will lead you to the turn markers. The main body of swimmers will collapse towards the markers and you can collapse right along with them and at the same time, stay out on the edge and away from all the traffic. Keep in mind that it gets very congested at the turn markers and it's best if you take a wide berth at all the turns.

As you are nearing the end of the swim the traffic will be thinned out and you can begin to edge closer to the course markers. The markers will lead you right to the beach area where you can get out of the water. Swim until your hand hits the bottom on the downstroke and then stand up. It's very difficult to walk or run in the water so keep swimming as long as you can.

If you use this swim strategy you will be swimming further, but you will be "swimming" for pretty much the whole course and not wasting time and effort fighting your way through all the traffic.

It's not so much about how fast you get to the finish of the swim, but *how* you get there and how you feel when you arrive that's most important. If your swim is controlled and enjoyable, then it will be reflected in your heart-rate. The anxiety of swimming in traffic and becoming scared, angry, or frustrated will increase your heart-rate and cause you to lose energy that will be unrecoverable for the rest of the race.

In every segment of this race remember that "pace is the key."

It simply can't be stressed enough.

How your swim turns out will greatly affect what happens in the run. You will certainly not recover energy you lose needlessly in the swim once you are out on the bike course. Once it's gone, it's gone for the race.

Swim within your abilities and try and avoid swimming as fast as you can so you can be a few minutes faster coming out of the water. There is little advantage to this unless you are a pro or top age-grouper and every single minute will count.

As you prepare for the gun to sound remind yourself that you have to pace yourself for three events and not just the swim. Above all, go into the swim with a plan and it will be a much more enjoyable experience. I truly hope you give serious consideration to what Terry had to say about "Total Immersion" because it could well be the answer to any anxiety you have about swimming. It is the ideal swimming strategy for not just conserving energy, but also for ensuring you have an enjoyable and successful triathlon swim.

41. THE SWIM-BIKE TRANSITION

When you first stand up at the end of your swim, it's quite common to be a bit dizzy. I believe there are two main reasons for this. First of all your body has been horizontal for some time and when you stand up your blood flow will take a few minutes to re-establish itself. However, I think there is a second reason that many people are unaware of.

If you seem to be "extra-dizzy" after some of your swims, it may be from water collecting in your ear canal. If this is a problem it will most likely reveal itself at some point in your training, and it would be worth trying ear-plugs during subsequent swims to see if it makes a difference.

If there are no wetsuit strippers available and you are on your own be sure to have a plan for getting your wetsuit off. It seems that the wetter a wetsuit is, the easier it is to get off. In other words, if you can find a spot that's out of the way soon after you exit the water, take your suit off there and carry it to your bike, instead of going to your bike with it on. This is especially true if your bike is a long distance away. If your bike is close to the exit from the water then take it off when you get to your bike.

You may also have success with this method:

Right before you stand up in the water, put your fingers in the collar of the wetsuit and pull it out so that it allows water to pour inside the suit. When you stand up, the water flushes through the suit from top to bottom and it make it easier to get the wetsuit off.

When you feel your hand hit bottom on your downstroke and first stand up, it's not really a good time to break into a full run. This will drive your heart-rate up when you would be better served to take your time and let yourself get oriented. *Walk* out of the water.

As you prepare to take your wetsuit off, it really helps if there is a post, side of a building, bike-rack, or other immovable object that you can lean against, as many people are still a bit dizzy and un-coordinated at this point. You can check this out before the swim start when you are looking over the transition area.

Leave your cap and goggles on until your wetsuit is off. This way you will keep your hands free. Unzip the suit completely, pull it down over your waist, and push it down to your ankles. Step on one side of the suit and pull that leg out, then step on the other side and pull the other leg out. It takes practice, but it does get easier. Carry your wetsuit to your bike and take your cap and goggles off as you walk over.

If wetsuit strippers are provided, then unzip your wetsuit as you approach them, and pull your wetsuit down past your knees and lay down. They will each grab a side and pull the suit off and hand it to you. Remember, your wetsuit, cap, and goggles are your responsibility.

Remember your pace. There is little benefit to be gained from running full out. All that will do is drive your heart-rate up and waste valuable energy. Walk steadily to your bike and get your thoughts organized. When you get to your bike tuck your wetsuit, goggles, and cap in a spot out of the way. Most shorter triathlons do not have change tents, so in most cases what you are wearing under your wetsuit is what you will be biking in. First of all, I hope that you remember to wear *something* under your wetsuit. Public nudity is not an option in any triathlon.

Don't forget your race number!

Personally, I used to attach my number to a number-belt and put it on under my wetsuit as I was already wearing my biking clothes. Be sure the number is facing to the back for the bike leg. They are waterproof, and I've never had a problem using this method.

If you are putting a biking top on *after* you get out of the water, don't forget to put your number belt on and turn it so it's on your back. Some people will pin their race numbers to their tops beforehand and wear it under their wetsuit that way. If you plan on wearing your biking clothes under your wetsuit, it would be a better idea to use a number belt whether you attach it before or after the swim and avoid pinning your number right on to your clothing. Pins are more likely to pop open if they are attached to your clothing because there is more flexing with your body movements. You don't really need the distraction of a race number flapping in the wind. So really, your number one choice should be a race belt.

Don't forget to put the food you have set aside for the bike leg in the pockets of your cycling jersey. Sometimes people realize 10 minutes after they leave transition that they forgot their food.

Once your bike shoes and helmet are on, take your bike out of the rack and *walk* toward the bike loading area.

Congratulations! Your triathlon swim is behind you, but for many new triathletes it's a much bigger story.

For many of those new to triathlon, making it through their first open water swim is very challenging. It's a big step and is quite an accomplishment for those who have to learn how to swim in order to compete in triathlons. It's another indication of just how much people are capable of when they begin to believe in themselves and never lose sight of their ultimate goal.

With so much of the planet being covered by water in the forms of lakes, rivers, oceans, ponds, and pools, learning to swim can one day be one of the most important things you take away from your foray into the world of triathlon. Basically it opens up a new world for you and will instill a confidence that may have significant impact on your life or the lives of others.

Just ask the three people involved when a young woman saw two older people several hundred meters from shore who had capsized their boat and were very near to drowning. She didn't hesitate and swam out to them and pulled them both to shore. When asked about it later she said....

"I knew I had to do something, and I also knew I had the training to do it because I just did a triathlon a few weeks ago".

Wow! That's pretty amazing when you think of alternative ways this story might have unfolded.

So as you leave the water after a successful swim and are making your way through transition toward your next challenge, you can be very proud of what you have accomplished and the progress you have made long before you even reach the finish line of your first triathlon.

42. THE BIKE COURSE

Be alert when you are walking your bike to the area designated for getting on your bike. It can get quite hectic and busy and often people are still a bit unsteady on their feet from the swim. I hope you remembered to leave your bike in a very easy gear before the race started. By having done this, you will make the initial meters of your bike ride much more controlled and as a result, far safer for you and those around you.

Also, I should mention this. I would never have thought of it, but just recently a guy who had just done his first triathlon was telling me how he had forgotten to take his swim cap off before putting his bike helmet on. He was out on the bike course for about 30 minutes and noticed how hot his head was getting. No kidding.

Well, the rule is, once you leave transition, you can't take off your bike helmet or you will be disqualified. The thinking is, that even if you are off your bike and standing on the side of the road with your helmet off, another cyclist or some other wayward vehicle could run into you and you won't have your head protected.

So he felt his only two options were to either bike all the way back to the transition area, take off his helmet and cap and start over again, or leave the cap on. So he left the swim cap on and got really hot, finished the race, and learned a valuable lesson.

Personally, I have never heard of this happening, but I can understand it happening in the chaos and confusion that often occurs when people try and make it through transition unnecessarily fast. In fact, he admitted that this exactly what he had done.

So just in case, pat your head before you put on your bike helmet. You never know.

As you are getting on your bike, be sure one shoe is locked into the pedal before you swing your other leg over and get on the bike. For instance, if you are mounting on the left side of your bike as most people tend to do, hold the bike steady and clip in your "left" foot. At least this will give you some control. It's not unusual to see new triathletes jump on a bike without first snapping in at least one pedal and then try maneuvering through transition traffic, while stabbing wildly at both pedals trying to get their shoes locked in. In the meantime their bike is weaving all over the place and everybody's ducking for cover.

If you are on the left side of your bike and make the mistake of clipping in your right foot first, I hope I'm there to get a picture of you sitting on your bike backwards or at least to witness the ensuing chaos. Yes, in the heat of battle that has happened before, but people I have seen do it realize their mistake almost right away and have to unclip that foot and clip in the other.

Once you have one shoe clipped in, it's a simple matter of pushing off with the other leg and mounting the bike and once you get some forward momentum, clip in the other shoe. Some people prefer to straddle their bike first and then clip in one shoe and then push off. Just practice both methods in training and see what works best for you.

When you yourself settled on your bike, start down the course and shift into the gear you're most comfortable with and bike in nice smooth circles. It's best to avoid eating and drinking for a while and let your body adjust to being out of the water and on the bike.

After about 15-20 minutes, take a drink, and if you choose to follow my earlier advice and have your watch pre-set to beep at regular intervals of 20 or 25 minutes, push the start button at this point. Or, if you prefer, you can start it the moment you get on your bike and just wait for the first beep to take your initial drink. As a rule in the first half of longer races I would drink at every beep and eat at every other one. In the last half of a shorter tri or last quarter of a longer tri, I would suggest you stop eating and keep on hydrating.

Of course the longer the triathlon is, the more important eating and drinking becomes. In a "try a tri" it may not be necessary to set your watch at all, as the short bike leg will be over quickly. If you have properly hydrated and carb-loaded in the days prior to a short tri, I don't expect you would need much to eat at all. In these shorter races, a banana, energy bar, or perhaps a few gels might be sufficient. However, as you stretch out your triathlons to the Olympic, Half-Ironman, and Ironman distances, a properly planned eating and hydration strategy cannot be over-stated..

Be sure you are aware of the regulations for drafting in the race you are in. Some shorter races may not stipulate one way or the other and some may say it's not an issue. However, once you get to the half-iron and Ironman distance, it's a very big issue and you will be penalized for drafting and possibly disqualified for doing it once to often. In races where drafting is not allowed, there will be course marshals on motorcycles who will be recording the race numbers of offenders.

The drafting zone is quite large, and you must stay a good three bike-lengths behind other cyclists unless you are overtaking and passing.

Once again the "pace is the key" in cycling, but also, "the spin is the key" as well. You always have to have in the back of your mind that you still have the run course up ahead. There is simply no benefit in being in the big chain-ring at the front of your bike unless you are going down quite a steep hill. Chances are, if you are a new triathlete cycling on the flat sections of the bike course in the big gear, you are *not* spinning and are over-taxing muscles you will need for the run.

Of course there will be exceptionally strong cyclists who are experienced bikers but perhaps new to triathlon who can handle bigger gears, but even they should be aware of the bike to run transition and how pushing big gears can cause problems later on. For most novice triathletes it's simply not the best course of action to be pushing bigger gears than necessary. Also be aware of the problems "over-spinning" can create. I often see this in the city when people are commuting to work on their mountain bikes. They are spinning furiously and hardly moving forward.

The reasoning may be that this saves energy. That may be true, but without at least *some* resistance it becomes very hard on your knees, and at the same time can be painful as everything in the knee mechanism is simply too loose if there is no resistance. Your knee goes "wonky" is a term that I have heard before.

Here is a good example....

I once had a discussion with a police officer I knew in town. She said she was on the police "Bike Patrol" that cruised the river pathway systems and other areas of the city that were not so accessible to police cruisers. I asked her how she liked it and she said it was great, but she might have to go back into cars because her knees hurt everyday. Right away I asked her if she did most of her riding in real easy gears and did she do a lot spinning at an extra-high rate. She said yes, because she thought it conserved energy. So I suggested to her to go into a gear big enough to

188

provide as least some resistance to her knees and still maintain a nice spin around 80-90 rpms. The next time I saw her a few weeks later, she said she was amazed, and that in just a day or two her knees felt better and never bothered her again.

So yes, the spin is the key, but it must be the right spin for you. This is what you should be working on in your bike training. Find that perfect gear (on the flats) that feels just right and is not so loose and you are spinning wildly at 100-110 rpms and not such a big gear that you are struggling to go 60 rpms. Try for somewhere between 80-90 rpms where there is *some* noticeable resistance, but yet it feels very good and within your ability. This is the main reason you should have a bike computer. It will tell you your rpms at any given time.

Once you have this figured out, you use your shifters to go into harder gears on the downhills and easier gears in the uphills. Do your best to maintain the same doable spin rate whether you are on the flats, or on upgrades or downgrades.

Of course on extremely big hills (like Richer's Pass in Penticton) there is often no gear small enough and you just do the best you can.

Always keep as far to the right of the road as you can unless you are passing. First of all, it's a race regulation, and secondly, nobody will surprise you and be able to pass you on your right. Passing on the right is dangerous and against regulations, but some people do it anyway. Maybe because the road is crowded or because they are not experienced and aware of this basic rule. If they are passing on the right and you move to the right at the same time, not aware that they are there, an accident can easily result. It's best to stay far enough to the right that it simply can't happen.

Also remember that it's dangerous and against regulations to bike over the center line. Often there will be vehicular traffic on the other side of the road and only one side is closed to traffic. It's a really dangerous thing to do. Even in cases (like around Skaha Lake in Penticton)where both sides of the road are close to regular vehicular traffic, it's still vitally important to stay on the right of the center line. That extra lane in used by emergency vehicles and course marshals and is out of bounds for racers.

In very small races, the road may not be closed at all and you are basically relegated to the shoulder of the road unless passing. In cases like this you must be extra cautious and aware of vehicular traffic.

Often it will get crowded at the bike aid stations. Try and make sure you have a buffer zone around you with no other cyclists close to your back or front, slow down, and pick up your food or water from the volunteers. Toss your empty water bottles in the designated areas at the aid stations and preferably not all over the bike course as the volunteers are responsible for cleaning up after you, so you can make their job much easier be being considerate though-out the course of the day.

When you are within 20 minutes or so of the bike to run transition, try standing up on the pedals and let your muscles become used to a different position as you will be off the bike and on your feet soon. Put a little pressure on one calf muscle and then the other by standing up on your toes. Do some shoulder shrugs as most likely your shoulder muscles will be tightened up a little. This is all perfectly normal and sometimes even a few simple stretches will make your transition into running a little easier as it will help to ease the "stiffness" in your muscles.

Of course, the longer the bike course, the more difficult the transition is from biking to running.

43. THE BIKE TO RUN TRANSITION

As you near the transition area you will be asked to *slow down*. Be sure you do, because no volunteer wants to try and catch a bike that's coming in at a break-neck speed.

Once you get off the bike, make your way through the transition area to the assigned slot where your bike belongs and where your running gear will be.

In longer races, volunteers will hand you your gear bag and take care of your bike as you head off to the change tent, but in shorter ones all your gear will be at your original bike station and you are responsible for your own bike. Be sure to leave your helmet on until you have your bike in its proper place.

In pretty well any triathlon of any length there will be medical personnel on hand in the transition area. If you have any problems this is the time to deal with them. For instance, maybe you fell off your bike and have some road rash or perhaps you just need a moment to catch your breath before beginning the run.

Most likely at a shorter triathlon you will have all your transition gear sitting near your spot on the bike rack. If there *are* change facilities, I always suggest to novice triathletes to change into clean dry running clothes at this point just to make their run a bit more comfortable. However this is often not the case so just go with the plan you put in place before the start of the race. If it's cool, this is the time to put on a jacket or sweater. If it's hot you may want to take off that jacket you wore during the bike.

Whatever you decide to wear, be sure to remember your race number. It goes on the front for the run, and not the back. If you are using a number belt as I suggested, it's a simple matter of sliding the belt around until the number is on your front. Remember, you only have to pin one number to your number belt, not two.

If it's very, very hot, I strongly suggest wearing a cap. You may also want to put on some sun-block if you feel you are going to be on the run course for some time. If you are using a fuel belt, this is also the time to put it on. It doesn't hurt to have a water bottle handy with your other gear in the event you want to start off your run with a drink of water. There's always the chance that the bottles on your bike will be empty.

I often see people carrying water bottles while they run, and this can become a nuisance very quickly. Your best bet by far is to use a fuel belt. Also, if you plan on taking along food, be sure you don't forget it. It's not even a bad idea to tape a checklist somewhere near your station as a reminder when you are making the transitions. Food, race-number, hat, sun-block, sunglasses, fuel belt, or anything else can go on your list, and just glance at it before you leave for the run. You can have two lists and do one for the swim-bike transition as well if you like.

Every race has it's own set of regulations. Be sure you read and understand them so you are fully aware of what will transpire in the transition zone.

Congratulations! You are doing amazingly well and are about to enter the final leg of your triathlon. Often it is at this point that many novice triathletes become fully aware that they are "really going to do it" and it's an exciting revelation.

Look how far you have come. Just look at you now. Maybe there was a time months or even years ago when this adventure seemed like a mountain too high or a finish line beyond your reach, yet as you put your running shoes on and are leaving transition for the final time you are beginning to realize the power of passion and resolve and how so much is within your reach if you are willing to go out and get it.

44. THE RUN

The way you feel when you leave the bike transition will all depend on how well you have prepared for the race.

If you have never practiced the bike-run transition, then you are in for a bit of an eye-opener. You are asking many muscles that helped propel you through the bike to now help get you through the run.

It only stands to reason that the longer the bike course was, the more impact it will have on your transition into the run. It's worth repeating that there are several things that can help make your triathlon run a more successful and pleasurable experience.

First of all, did you stick to the plan of "spinning" on your bike and not overdoing it with big gears? Did you eat and drink the proper amounts in relation to the length of the event? Did you practice the bike to run transitions in the weeks and months leading up to the race?

These are all extremely important considerations that will have an impact on your run experience on race day.

If it's your very first tri you should have a plan in place long before the race as to how you intend to approach the run. Do you intend to run most of it? Do you intend to walk most of it? Or perhaps you adopted my idea of having a "run-walk" strategy in mind.

I would say "run-walk" would be my number one preference for the novice triathlete. Even just running a minimum amount in your first triathlon is a great accomplishment.

Maybe in your very first triathlon you will walk for 8 minutes and run easily for 1 or 2. There's nothing wrong with that for a starting point. If during the course of the race you feel really good you can always shorten the walk and extend the run. To me, it seems like the ideal format and gives you so much control out on the run course.

Over time you will find yourself running more and walking less as you continue on with your triathlon career and become fitter and fitter as time goes by.

I have noticed over the years that many people have stomach issues during the run portions of a triathlon. Of course this is more prevalent in the longer races, but it's a good idea to develop sound eating and drinking strategies early in your career and you initial shorter races are a great testing ground.

Most digestive problems seem to develop from having no real plan in place as far as eating and drinking. So what generally happens is that triathletes try pretty much any foods or drinks that are available at the aid stations in the hopes of making themselves feel better. It's a slippery slope.

For instance, at Ironman Canada you might have a choice of gels, bananas, cookies, energy bars, grapes, cantaloupe, chicken soup, Gatorade, water, or flat pop. By the time many people are at mile 12 they have already tried a bit of everything looking for that magic "feel good" bullet that simply does not exist. Their energy has gone AWOL and it's nowhere to be found no matter what they force into their bodies.

So it's little wonder that people have stomach issues. For one thing, they are most likely eating foods they never, ever ate in training. I have yet to see a cantaloupe bulging out of a cyclists jersey pocket.

I know exactly how these people are feeling and I know what they're attempting to do by eating and drinking out of control, because I made all those same mistakes myself before I wised up.

The secret to feeling great on the run begins way back at the start of the bike course. That's the time to take in the complex carbohydrates (like a bagel with peanut butter and honey), for example. Whatever you are eating on the bike, it's important that you've eaten it in training and *know* it agrees with you. Eat these complex carbohydrates early on in the bike as it will take your body longer to assimilate them, and that's what you want at this stage. You want *long lasting* fuel, not something like a gel that goes straight into your bloodstream. Save those for later on in the bike if you feel you need a short burst of energy.

It you were to eat two bagels 15 minutes before the end of the bike ride with the assumption that this would help you in the run, you would be making a critical mistake. You body will be trying to assimilate it while you are running and it just won't have the time. Eating that late does you little good and actually *overtaxes* your digestive system at a critical point in the race. Often this will cause triathletes to "bonk" and simply run out of energy.

In other words, what they were attempting to do had the exact opposite result.

I really believe that if you eat the proper foods (foods that are slowly assimilated) early on in the bike, and keep your glycogen levels on an even keel, and do not take on food in the *late* stages of the bike, you will be setting yourself up nicely for the run. Regardless of whether you are in an Olympic or Ironman distance race, most likely all you will need is water at regular intervals in the run and very little, or no food at all if you have done things just right.

This will do wonders for your digestive system and make your run experience much more enjoyable.

You also want to maintain a hydration strategy that ensures you are drinking *small amounts* on a steady, controlled basis (use your timer), and not large amounts once in a while at uncontrolled intervals during the bike and this will pay dividends in the run where you will maintain the same drinking plan.

All of this adds up to a great experience, and you will be in full control of your run and can really enjoy yourself while you interact with other athletes, volunteers, and spectators you run into all the way.

This is a big moment in your life. In a short time you will realize the crowning glory of all the work you have done to get yourself to this point.

As you enter the final kilometer of the run course, you will most likely see more and more spectators along the course cheering you on.

As the finish line appears in your sights and you cross over what is perhaps your very first triathlon finish line, you might see family and friends who have been your support team and are there to share in your huge accomplishment.

It is truly an amazing moment that will surely have a huge impact on your life.

You have discovered just how much you are truly capable of, and the more you had to overcome to get to this point, the more profound this defining moment in your life will be.

45. REFLECTIONS

He was hooked the moment he turned on the television and landed on ABC's coverage of the 1982 Hawaii Ironman. It was the first time he'd ever set eyes on a triathlon. It didn't matter that he couldn't swim a stroke and had a fear of the water. It didn't matter that the last bike he'd ever been on was over twenty years ago as a teen. Despite everything, the finish line of the Hawaii Ironman was calling him so clearly that it might as well of been in his living room screaming in his ear.

It was early in 1983 when it all began with his very first swim instructor saying in her sweet patient voice, "well, if you plan on doing this Ironman thing, you're gonna' have to let go of the side of the pool" to six months later when he swam non-stop for two miles in the local pool with the swim stroke from Hell. It was all the encouragement he needed to send in his entry for Ironman Hawaii 1984 as a foreign contestant. It was a category created by the Ironman organizers to make the Hawaii Ironman an International event, and Americans were already on a wait list. All too soon his acceptance arrived in the mail and his journey into the unknown began.

The weeks and months flew by in a heartbeat, and he found himself sitting out on the lanai of his condo the eve of Hawaii Ironman 1984. He had a perfect view of Kona harbor and the small boats that scurried back and forth as they jockeyed the bright-colored swim course markers into place. "You can stop anytime now" he thought as they pulled the buoys further and further out from shore. His first open water swim was going to take him 1.2 miles out from shore before he would make the turn back to the bike transition. He watched as the "Captain Bean" boat with her bright orange sails was brought to anchor at the turn. "What have I gotten myself into?" he thought as the self-doubt began to creep in.

His tortured sleep that night was punctuated by the roar of the surf crashing against the shore and his lullaby the voices of the Iron Gods challenging him on the warm Hawaiian winds that snuck in through the sliding glass doors. "So! You want to be an Ironman! We're waiting for you. Do you have what it takes?"

The restless night passed in a blur and suddenly it's thirty minutes from the swim start and he's pumping his tires to around the 100 PSI mark that everyone seemed to think was about right. The mantra around Kona in previous days had been "don't pump up your tires the night before because they'll expand and explode in the humidity of the Hawaiian night." Pump, pump, POW, and his tube exploded into shreds. "Thanks guys, that was a great plan." No time for panic ... put on your spare. The thought crossed his mind that even before his bike wheel did one revolution of the 112 mile bike course he was putting on his only spare tube. "Just great," he thought. "I can't risk another flat or my day is over. I'll just put in 60 lbs of air instead of 100."

It's a surreal moment. Thousands of spectators, volunteers, T.V. crews, and athletes in total silence as the priest blesses the event, the only sound the spinning rotors of the five media helicopters hovering over the harbor waiting to record the mass swim start of an Ironman, one of the most amazing sights in the world of sports. Instinctively he knew that this was a moment in time that would be burned into his memory forever.

Suddenly the cannon sounds and in an instant he's swept away in a wild, churning cauldron of flailing arms and legs. Everywhere he turned he swam into someone and yet he had never felt so alone. Swallowing mouthfuls of briny water and fighting back the panic he rode the swells up and down, his arms sometimes missing the water and grabbing only air. Then like magic he was free, and a stunning visual display spread out below him. Schools of blue, green, red, and yellow tropical fish danced beneath him in weaving, swaying, darting patterns. Scuba divers sitting on the ocean floor waved up at him. Onward, onward he swam, moving his arms as fast as he could and not daring to stop or slow down for fear of being sucked down into the depths.

In those first few furious minutes he had swum further than he ever had in his life without having the end of a pool to hang on to. "One more marker, one more marker" he said over and over again to himself and then like magic, there it was, the big boat with the orange sails and a surge of energy coursed through him as he heard a multitude of voices urging him on from the deck. With one last stroke he pulled himself around the stern of the "Captain Bean" boat, tried his best to smile for the underwater photographer who was taking his picture, and made the turn for home.

He feels a surge of elation as the current lifts him and carries him toward shore. Faster and faster the bright round markers pass by and disappear in the distance behind him. The huge inflated can of Bud Light Beer that marked the end of the swim course was growing bigger and bigger. Never had a can of beer looked so good. Then he was there! He saw knees and ankles all around him as volunteers pulled him to his feet and pushed him toward dry land and into the change tent where you could cut the relief with a knife and the atmosphere was euphoric and he realized the swim was a challenge for many others as well. The swim is soon a distant memory as he steers his trusty bike with the squishy tires through Kona and out into the sweltering heat of the King K. highway.

106, 108, 110 degrees the temperature continues to climb as the day wears on and a long line of cyclists fight the sweltering heat, the torrid winds, and the demons that urge them to "stop right now and it will all be over! Stop and you can go back to your room and rest!" On and on he cycled, with each downstroke of the pedals the soft tires sink into the super-heated asphalt. "112 miles," he thought. "This bike with two squishy tires has to get me through 112 miles."

His feet begin to swell against the toe-clips and every revolution of the tires send darts of pain coursing through his legs. Every fiber of his body shouts at him to STOP and on and on he pedals into the shimmering heat waves that seemed to dance higher and higher off the lava-wrapped highway with each passing mile. Fleeting images of beautiful Hawaiian girls in grass skirts and flowers in their hair holding out cool sponges and guava jelly sandwiches on brown bread and how remarkably easy it was to confuse the two. Every time the road turned, the relentless headwind seemed to shift with it, and yet the worst was still to come.

Then he is there, the big climb to Hawi and the turn for the long trip back. Now the sea winds howl in earnest and try to push him off the road as he climbs and climbs and climbs.

"I can't go on, I can't do anymore!" he screams inside, and the voices of the Iron Gods in the relentless wind taunt him. "Is that all you've got!" they howl. "IS THAT ALL YOU'VE GOT!"

Facing the abyss his thoughts drift back to the finish line that called him to so long ago. "Hang on to your dream. No matter what, hang on to your dream," he thought, and he willed himself over the crest of the hill, made the turn, and gloried in the relief as the big uphill was now his friend and urged him on and gave him strength to fight his way back home. Back into Kona and out again with still more bike-work to do. Down, down into the Pit and the final stop for his steadfast bike. A miracle, a true miracle, that it never let him down and carried him all the way through Hell and back home again.

One last change and the run begins with the ascent from "the Pit" and all thoughts of a strong, fast marathon are quickly laid to rest and become a distant memory. Up, up with screaming muscles out of the pit and down the highway to Kona and out of town once more to face the inferno of the King K. Highway one last time. Run then walk, run then walk, onward, onward with each step drawing him closer to the impossible dream.

In the distance a welcome site as the final turn is near. Volunteers are cheering now, "the last turn!" they yell, "just 13 more miles to go!"

"Oh my God! It's just too far!" but still he shuffles onward. From light to dark and hot to cool the Hawaiian night sneaks in. Faceless shapes they come and go, mere shadows in the dusk. A band of weary warriors all together, yet alone. Lime-green light sticks spring to life and sparkle in the night. Bobbing and weaving in the dark as far as the eye can see. Forlorn figures sit or lay on the edges of the road. There's nothing left, there is no more and the blaze of flashing lights and screaming sirens pierce the island night and another one is gone and will fight no more today.

He wants to reach out and touch his Iron comrade and say "you're a hero just for being here, there is no loser and no failing today," but forward, ever forward he stumbles into the night struggling with the sadness he feels for those who have come so far only to fall just short, and the overwhelming pain and tiredness that envelopes him as he wills one weary foot in front of the other.

When all hope seems lost, a glimmer appears on the distant horizon. Soon the glimmer brightens until it becomes a steady glow that becomes more luminous with each tortured shuffling and stumbling step forward. Like a beacon in the night guiding mariners adrift in an endless sea, he realized he was seeing the lights of Kona calling him home.

On and on he forced himself forward and everywhere now he heard people calling out in the night. "Keep going! You're going to make it! It's not far now! You're going to be an Ironman soon!" The lights glowed brighter and brighter and more and more spectators line the route as he reaches the outskirts of town.

The streets of Kona are filled with spectators and their shouts of support and growing crescendo of applause give him strength to push onward farther and farther into town. One more step, one more building, and then one more block pass behind him and his vision is blurry as he feels the tears filling his eyes when he catches a glimpse of Kona harbor just ahead.

Now there are cheering people everywhere, but he is all alone on the road. He looks down the street and glances behind and there is nobody in his sight. The sea-wall looms ahead and then he's there. One more right-hand turn onto Ali'i Drive and it takes his breath away.

The magic of the moment is seared into his memory and for an instant, time stands still. Up ahead a row of huge, bright lights shine down on the finish. He remembers now that it's the ABC camera lights that he saw shining down on the finishers on his television an eternity ago. Throngs of spectators line the sea-wall and wait to bring him home. He is overcome by the magnitude of what is about to transpire. All that has been wrong in his life is about to become right. He marvels that his body brought him so far. It has forgiven his transgressions. It holds no malice for the abuse he heaped on it by years of smoking, drinking, and the careless disregard of his youth. It has welcomed and nurtured his efforts to become stronger, fitter, and more in tune with the Universe. The sea is calm and the throngs are silent as a gust of wind engulfs him in a warm embrace. The Iron Gods are back. But now he feels their pleasure and their once challenging shouts are a welcome whisper in his ear.

"Aloha. Aloha Ironman. Welcome home."

With a surge of energy, he charges toward the finish straight. The aches and pains, and fears and doubts are distant memories as the sea crashes on the shore and the crowd calls out to him. "Ironman! You are an Ironman!

The dream that seemed so distant and so impossible is coming true. On into the blinding lights he runs and as he sees the finish line pass beneath his feet he knows his life has somehow changed and will never be the same again.

46. DREAMING, BELIEVING, AND ACHIEVING

There are so many reasons why the challenging sport of triathlon has turned so many lives around. By its very nature, it requires you to develop skills that are completely new to you, and in the learning and fine-tuning of these skills you improve yourself on so many levels that reach far beyond the physical.

As difficult as the challenge may be, it remains within the grasp of so many people; so many extraordinary, ordinary people. The sport does not demand that you be a super athlete, live in a certain part of the world, or be in the prime of your youth. It is not reserved for only the wealthy, the cultured, or the ultra-educated. It does not care is you are a Japanese farmer, a Baker from Indianapolis, or a mom of three from the West Coast.

It simply does *not* care.

All the sport of triathlon cares about is *do you have it within you to answer the challenge and take your life in a vibrant, exciting, new direction?*

Often the journey to distant finish lines can be cloaked in the shadows of self-doubt, yet with each small step forward, with each tiny victory, glimmers of light will one day burst into a luminous, everlasting glow and you will realize that indeed, the spirit within you will sing if only you give it a chance.

The devotion and hard work required to become skillful and confident in swimming, biking, and running is an amazing accomplishment for so many, yet the true victory is in the dreaming, believing and achieving of all the things in this life that seem to be beyond our reach.

Take up the challenge and long after the cheers grow silent, your brilliant accomplishments will continue to resonate within you. You will look back to that magic moment when you were stirred into action and resolved to make a change in your life, and you will be in awe when you realize how far you have come and just how much you are truly capable of.

All of the amazing people who have contributed to this book have a passion for what they do and to me passion is the main ingredient for success in this world. It seems that no matter what a person aspires to or dreams of, if the passion is never lost, success is always within reach.

I truly hope that the knowledge, wisdom, and passion we have shared with you inspires you to chase your dreams and make that transition from the sidelines of life to a resolute and passionate traveler on the highway of magnificent accomplishments where dreams really do come true.

The End